# Contents

*The purpose of this book is to teach you to survive!*

## My Many Thanks

I would like to thank all my many friends and professional advisers, who have helped me in the writing of this book;

My wife Vera, for the many hours spent correcting my notes and piecing together all the information;

My two sons, Eddie and Perry, who spent many, many hours of hard work helping me to set up lectures, up and down the country;

Miss Audrey Whitehead, who patiently typed and corrected my many hundreds of scrap paper notes;

Mr. Paul Crompton, for taking this process further;

The friends that I have made while serving in the Army for their patience and confidence at all times,

The Press for the excellent publicity they have given me over the years;

And finally, the man who made this book possible, who throughout gave me great encouragement and the confidence to sit down and compile it, Lt. Col. John Blashford Snell M.B.E. R.E., to me the World's greatest living explorer, a great leader and a great man.

◇

# NO NEED TO DIE

Real Techniques of Survival

◇

**Eddie McGee**

◇

**PAUL H. CROMPTON LTD.**
638, Fulham Road,
London, S.W.6.
England.

1st Edition 1978
2nd Edition 1982
2nd Edition Reprinted 1982

I.S.B.N. 901764 — 41 — 8
Printed in England By Elsworth Bros. Ltd.,
Bowman Lane, Leeds, LS10 1JD.
Illustrated by the Author.

## Survival Psychology

The definition of the word Survival in the dictionary reads:

**Survivor:**    One who lives when others die.

**Survival:**    To fight to live on when all help has gone.

Man's urge to survive and refuse to die when the odds are stacked against him is unique. The ability to do the things which would normally be meaningless to him are also unique, especially once he has got over the fear of the unknown.

The greatest killers are:
COLD        WET        WIND

No matter what the weather in the desert, polar cap, jungle or even on the sea, man's ingenuity can overcome all. Fear soon changes to shock, shock to anger, and anger to disgust. Disgust at being caught out. When all these emotions have passed then man's ability to survive takes over. He becomes a **SURVIVOR.**

## THE ENEMIES OF THE SURVIVOR ARE:

INJURY — HUNGER — THIRST — DISEASE
COLD — HEAT — FEAR — LONELINESS
PANIC — ANGER — LACK OF TEACHING
LACK OF CONFIDENCE

## AIDS TO MAN'S SURVIVAL ARE:

PHYSICAL CONDITION

LOCAL KNOWLEDGE

EQUIPMENT

AND MOST IMPORTANT OF ALL

### THE WILL TO SURVIVE

# 1   Some basics of survival

When I was young I remember reading an article in the local paper about a farmer who had been chased by a bull and escaped because he had taken off his coat and dropped it while running away. The bull turned on the coat and began tearing and stamping, taking its fury out on the garment, thus giving the farmer time to escape. Thirty years later I was to experience the same danger myself. It happened whilst I was serving in the army in the north of England. At the time I was crossing one of the fields near the camp while out on one of my daily nature walks. As always I had on my old army Burgon type rucksac. In fact I never went anywhere without it. I used to like the feel of the pack on my back because it always gave me a sense of security, plus the fact that I had inside the pack all my survival bits and pieces and my ever-faithful brewing kit without which I would never travel anywhere.

On this particular day I was strolling across the field watching some rabbits playing around on top of a small crest near one side of the field. Busy in my thoughts I had not bothered to look at the other side of the field and so had not noticed the bull slowly walking towards me. About two hundred yards ahead of me was an old oak tree that I often used to sit under and sketch and indeed once again I seemed to be making for the tree though I know not why on this day, for it was in fact blowing quite hard and there was quite a bit of a nip in the air. However, towards it I went and when I think about it now, because of the regularity of my visits it in fact saved my life on this day. Had I been going straight across the field, then I certainly would not have heard the bull dashing towards me. In fact, I would have been walking straight into the wind. Suddenly I heard this noise of pounding hooves and grunting. Turning I saw the bull about four to five hundred yards away coming in my direction. Fortunately, the bull was not in full gallop but, I think, had just started to run. I realised immediately that the charge was meant for me and I remember to this day quite clearly that I did not panic but very casually slipped one of the shoulder straps of the rucksac off my shoulder and started to stride out towards the old tree. Remembering something I had learnt from an old poacher friend of mine I tried to get the tree, bull, and myself in

one straight line, knowing that the bull, like most animals, worked on movement and shape.

Keeping this in mind I now quickened my own pace and made hard towards the tree. I knew that it was useless with the pack on to try to out-run the bull across the field towards the gate or hedge. At this stage I dropped my rucksac, throwing it out of the line of the tree. The trick worked. The bull saw the new shape and started towards it rather than me and once I had reached the tree I simply but slowly moved to the rear of it. The bull had reached the rucksac and really began to knock hell out of it and standing where I was I could hear all its fury being put into tossing and stamping all over my rucksac. For myself, I was in no real danger now for just above me was a big strong branch on which many a time I had sat when on my walks watching the young wild animals below running and playing. The bull continued to tear and smash at my rucksac for a good few minutes so I thought the time had come for me to seek new safety. Reaching up slowly, I pulled myself up into the tree and made myself safe. I knew there was no sense in shouting at the bull to get off. One, I did not think it would hear me and two, I did not want it coming over to the tree and having a go at me. There was no sense in enraging the animal further so I just sat and watched. In fact it was a good fifteen minutes before the bull began to tire of the rucksac and I can tell you I'm glad that I was not on the receiving end of the bull. Once tired and satisfied it had done its deed, the bull began to paw the ground for a couple of seconds then galloped off across the field away from the tree. Twenty minutes later using the same survival skills as before I dropped from the tree keeping it between me and the bull and slowly moving backwards away from the tree I retrieved my rucksac and continued my walk backwards away from the bull. When about a hundred yards from the hedge I turned around and slowly walked on. Once on the other side of the hedge I had a good look around to assure myself that no other bulls were in the next field. Once satisfied I had a good look at my Burgon and what a shock I had. Anything that was breakable in it was broken and trampled beyond use or repair. So a little thought and common sense saved my life probably on that day.

Everyone knows about Scout Knots and Lashings, yet how many of us have actually ever sat and practiced them. Daily we read of ancient digs going on around us regularly turning up old tools and other oddments that our forefathers used to survive with before modern mechanisation came along. Our museums are filled with some excellent examples, and some of the methods and items used then are not far from some of the methods we use today.

There are very few of us in this country anyway who can honestly say that they have actually sat down to make tools for themselves. It is too easy for us to simply get up and go out and buy what we need.

Within this chapter I have tried to simplify some of the common tools that the survivor may need. Not necessarily in order of priority though. Simple ideas that the survivor may find useful to him and help ease his daily chores.

Tools for hunting, trapping, fishing, cooking, medicine and tools for making other tools, all simple yet greatly used by the survivor.

Included in this chapter is the art of packing your rucksac; a thing that many professional walkers and climbers do not know how to do correctly.

There is also a mention of home made survival packs. Simple yet very useful to the survivor should he be caught out without any aids or equipment. This particular piece of information is probably the most important part of the whole book. Something that every adventurer, or survivor must know before he attempts to embark on any expedition, or adventure.

I am often asked by the people who want to go on various expeditions, safaris etc., "What do you recommend in the way of a good knife, or a matchet?" and my answer to this is to show them a very wide selection of assorted knives and matchets that I have acquired over the years travelling around.

I think like all travellers I have a certain preference for certain things that I carry around with me, and a favourite knife is no exception.

Below I have listed a few points, for and against, for the knives that I have used around the world (in fairness to the manufacturers though, I'm the first to admit that each knife has its own merits and that improper use is probably the worst enemy here). However, in the case of the survivor the knife to be used must have certain qualities and these are strength, correct length, adaptability, a good point, be sharpened at least on one side and an extra

bonus is that the handle should be made in such a way that it can help the knife float by giving the knife a buoyancy, and if the knife handle is hollow then certain survival requisites can be stored in it. There is such a knife on sale, but unfortunately the handle is made of soft steel and the blade of the knife itself is not very robust and strong.

Another important feature of the knife is that it must have a good strong sheath or cover to protect it when not in use.

It is pointless taking a knife under six inches in blade length into the jungle. From my own experience I have found that the ideal length of blade that I can best work with anywhere in the world is the ex-army Parang. This is about sixteen inches long including the handle, the actual blade being eleven inches long. It is beautiful and strong, extremely sharp, has an excellent case cover. I had a few minor alterations to mine, like a saw set of two inches on the upper blade, a moulded handle of rubber over the existing wooden handle, and a small skinning knife and sharpening stone added to the outer case. Moulded into the rubber handle are some fish hooks and small compass, needle, cotton, matches and a razor blade. Once again giving me full survival protection should I ever need it.

## WOOD

The presence of any type of tree, shrub or bush, tells the survivor many things.

**Trees and plants** need water to survive.

**Trees and plants** only grow up to a certain level (known as the tree line).

**Trees and plants** provide food for man and animals, tools, fuel and medicines.

**Trees and plants** provide shelter, markers, aids and tell you the season and directions.

In my own experience I have found that some knowledge of herbal and tree recognintion in this country has proven invaluable to me when I have travelled in other countries. Traps built here, for instance for rabbitting work just as well in Africa, or the Oman, for catching other game. Once you have learned how to dice, stew, or cook roots and herbs etc., here in England, it is surprising how easily you adapt the same thing in other countries, once you have recognised a few plants. In Africa for instance I found the pygmies prepare their potatoes exactly as we do here, by boiling.

At this stage it would not go amiss if I mentioned a few helpful survival tips I learnt while on my travels. In fact I must admit I have used some of the ones taught me here in England and in the other countries.

Did you know for instance, that if you cut up small chunks of apple and put these on your hooks they make excellent bait? And many's the time I have snared duck and other water fowl by this method.

Honey cone makes an excellent delayed type of bait. By that I mean, instead of putting it directly on to the hook, break off small pieces and sprinkle on the water up-stream from the hook. A couple of seconds later it will start to break up and sink down to the bottom thus attracting the fish.

Try pulling off some old rotten bark from an old tree; you will be surprised at the amount of small but edible grubs you will find (edible to the fish that is). Once again crumble this up and drop it in the water above your hook.

## Let's consider a tree for example

1. The young leaves of most common trees provide a food source.
2. Young saplings and twigs provide materials for traps and weapons.
3. Most trees have a strong and weak side to the survivor; this helps him with his directions (not so in the jungle!)
4. The outer bark of most trees when boiled for twelve hours and diluted can be used for constipation, except the yew, laburnum and rhododendron.
5. The inner bark of all European trees is very nutritious, especially the pine. (Not so the yew, laburnum and rhododendron).
6. All tree wood burns and floats, including the great Burma teak.
7. Rotted wood invariably provides many species of insects useful to the survivor for fishing and setting of traps.
8. A tree like a fire to a survivor is a great morale booster.

## Useful survival hints

### DON'T

1.  Use stones from rivers or damp walls to surround fires. (They will crack when hot and often explode).
2.  Use large logs, wet logs, or build flat profile fires.
3.  Camp too near to cliff edges.
4.  Camp too near rivers or swampy ground. You will be pestered by insects, will spoil all game tracks, be open to possible flooding, be on damp ground and have difficulty in obtaining a dry fuel supply for your fire.
5.  Take water from the edge of a stream, river, pond or lake.
6.  Eat anything that gives off a foul smell or looks inedible.
7.  Eat roots or plant stems that contain a white milky substance or sap.
8.  Eat animals not caught by you.

### DO

1.  Get a fire going as soon as possible (a fire is a great morale booster).
2.  When cooking, try to use one of the following woods for fuel.
3.  Remember — Nothing ventured, nothing gained.

ASH

OAK

BEECH

PINE

HOLLY

HAWTHORN

# Making Tools from Wood

One of the best natural woods around for making tool handles and indeed in some cases the actual tools themselves is the every day common old tree Ivy.

This is excellent insomuch as it has in many cases natural bends in it especially if the wood has been climbing around a tree or such.

When the wood is still alive, or indeed has just been cut then it is very supple indeed and can be bent quite easily into all manner of weird shapes before it actually dries out. Also the wood is very easy to work with and very clean.

Spoons, forks and even wooden knives can be made from this wood. The making of pick handles, axe shafts etc., are also very easy because the wood

itself is so easy to work with. Therefore, it is one of the easiest woods from which to learn carving. Once dried out it dries to beautiful white, and when dried it becomes very hard and durable.

Should you be fortunate enough to be able to get hold of a good old very thick trunk type branch of Ivy then you can make excellent containers i.e. cups, saucers, bowls etc. In my barn at home I still have a very old hay rake made from Ivy and to my knowledge it is over two-hundred and eighty years old now and is still in excellent condition.

Whilst in the far east I noticed that the Malayans used lots of tree Ivy for making tools and even for certain jobs around the house i.e. roof lays, supports, and even door archways.

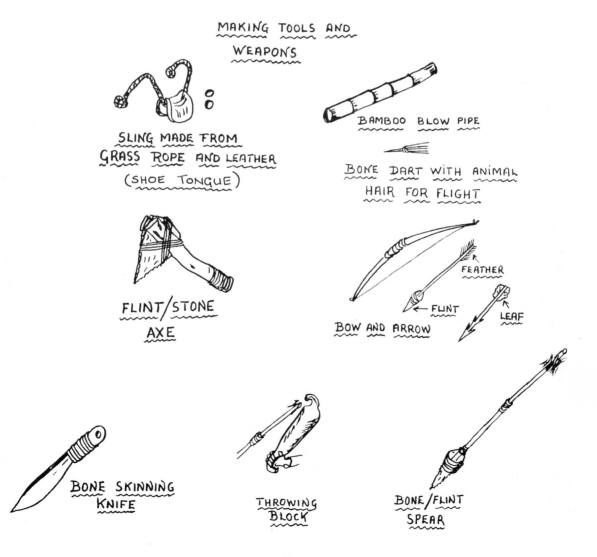

MAKING TOOLS AND WEAPONS

SLING MADE FROM GRASS ROPE AND LEATHER (SHOE TONGUE)

BAMBOO BLOW PIPE

BONE DART WITH ANIMAL HAIR FOR FLIGHT

FLINT/STONE AXE

FEATHER

FLINT

LEAF

BOW AND ARROW

BONE SKINNING KNIFE

THROWING BLOCK

BONE/FLINT SPEAR

# SOME NATIVE TOOLS AROUND THE WORLD

GRINDING STONE
AND BLOCK – OMAN

WOODEN CARVED SPOON

WORLD WIDE

AUSTRALIAN
FISHING
SPEAR

AUSTRALIAN
STONE CHISEL

AFRICAN DIGGING

STICK

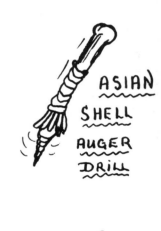

ASIAN
SHELL
AUGER
DRILL

SKIMMING SPOON
MADE FROM BAMBOO
AFRICAN

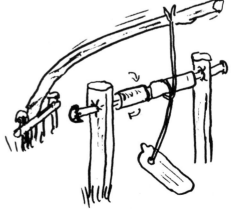

ANCIENT
WOOD LATHE

## Useful Tools and Aids

The need for aids to your every day survival are a must and the more time and effort you can put into the making of the tools the easier and it is going to be for you. Start off by making the basic essentials. Something to fish with if you are lucky enough to be near water. On land it is important that you have a good tool for digging.

Tools for your trap making, and of course for your cooking needs. Nearly always one needs some kind of container, be it either to collect water or food supplies in, or simply to store food. In both cases for the survivor the time will come when you find the need for a container. So set about making one or finding one as soon as you can.

The common every-day hand corn grinder that we see being used is also a very handy thing, not only for grinding corn but for the grinding of herbs and other spices that you may have grown or collected.

In the Middle East my grinding stone used to act two fold. When not grinding corn, etc. then I would use it for the purpose of washing. By this I mean I used to take it down to the sea with me and use it for beating out my washing on, as the beach was nothing but pure sand.

A must for anyone, be he survivor or simply camper is a spoon or ladle of sorts. You will find this will have a million uses around the camp, not only in cooking, but for tasting and collecting. In fact it would be safe for me to say, make two or three of varying sizes. They will always come in useful.

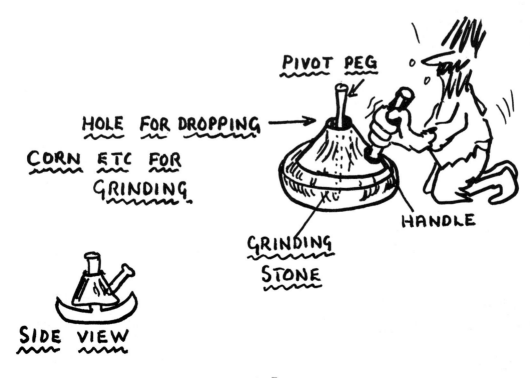

PIVOT PEG

HOLE FOR DROPPING CORN ETC FOR GRINDING

GRINDING STONE

HANDLE

SIDE VIEW

## A Simple Survival Pack

Over the years that I have been teaching survival, I have often been asked "What do you recommend to make up a basic survival pack?" so below I have listed what I consider essentials. I have not placed them in any order of importance as I feel each one is just as important as the other, and indeed in some cases they double up on each other.

## My Recommended Basic Survival Pack List.

Pencil and paper. Razor blades (2), needle and cotton, safety and straight pins, reflector glass, fish hooks, line weights, plastic water (balloon) bag, rubber bands, small compass, candle, windproof matches, hacksaw blade, (sharpened at one end, and shaped at the other for use as a screwdriver,) snare wire, whistle, glucose and salt tablets and if possible a small booklet on survival.

Your pack container must not be too large or indeed too heavy and with careful packing and the right choosing of the contents you should be able to get all your items into a tin about the size of a cigarette packet. A good practice here is to carry a spare candle with you. With this you can waterproof your container, and your matches. To do this, warm the lid, scrape the candle along the inside of lid edge, now put the lid back on, run the candle along the join, now the tin is waterproof.

It is also possible to make an excellent survival pack using the same contents and squeeze them into a match box. If you do use this method you will have to waterproof the matches individually. This is a simple task. Melt some of the candle wax in the bottom, lay a layer of matches in the wax pressing them gently into the wax. now melt a bit more of the wax over the matches. This will make an excellent seal, but do not forget this method will not make the matches windproof.

At this stage it is well to remember that you can easily find yourself carrying too much kit, the object of this pack is simply a safety pack to be used only in the event of an emergency, so it is essential that careful selection of the items be done at this point. Weight and bulk must be carefully controlled.

## Packing Your Rucksack

| LEFT FOR FOOD | RIGHT FOR LIFE |
|---|---|
| Oxo, Soups, Matches | Matches, Asprin/Codeine |
| Chocolate | Field Dressing |
| Mess Tins | Bandage, Plasters |
| Milk, Sugar, Tea | Razor Blade, Compass |
| Knife, Fork, Spoon | Whistle, Torch (Spare Battery) |
| Glucose | Chalk, Penknife, Snare Wire |
| Sweets | Hacksaw Blade, Reflector Glass |
| Water Bottle | Fish Hooks, Line, Candle |
| Plastic Bag | Pencil and Paper |

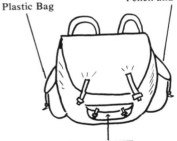

TOILET KIT
Soap, Towel etc,
Foot powder, Insect Repellent

## Always pack in reverse order First in Last out.

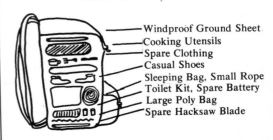

Windproof Ground Sheet
Cooking Utensils
Spare Clothing
Casual Shoes
Sleeping Bag, Small Rope
Toilet Kit, Spare Battery
Large Poly Bag
Spare Hacksaw Blade

## A Poacher's Whistle

Not only is the poacher's whistle a useful aid to the survivor for his food supply but for entertainment purposes it can be a great morale booster.

I was taught how to make a whistle when I was very young by my father, and I can remember the many happy hours I used to have as a boy, sitting and waiting for the rain to stop, puffing and blowing like mad trying to get some kind of a tune from it.

As I mention many times in the book, boredom is one of the worst enemies of the survivor. Anything to occupy your mind during the long wait that you may have to encounter is a must and I found if I ever did get myself into a state that I needed to sit and mope then I used to try to occupy myself by making things that would be of interest and indeed usefulness to my very survival. The old poacher's whistle always seemed to crop up. Not always did I succeed. But nine times out of ten my efforts drove away my low ebb.

I have mentioned that the best type of wood used here in Europe is the Sycamore tree. This type of wood is very common here in Europe and indeed plentiful. I personally know of no other kind of soft wood which peels its bark so easily for this purpose, though I must confess I did once make a whistle from elderberry but only after one or two disastrous failures.

## How to Make a Poacher's Whistle

The best type of wood for this is Sycamore, preferably when it is young and fresh. Early spring is a good time to get hold of the right wood.

## How to do it

1. Cut yourself a length of Sycamore about 6" long and an inch thick. This is about the right thickness for you to practise with.

2. Very gently score around the stem about 2" from the end cutting the bark.

3. Now twist firmly but gently the 2" section (but before you do this you need to cut in a small 'v' section as shown in the diagram) and remove.

4. Scrape the end section as shown and place the 2" bark section back on. You should now have a Poacher's whistle complete. With practise you can acquire excellent animal noise imitations.

# KNOTS AND LASHINGS

## REEF KNOT

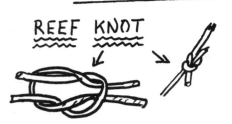

FOR JOINING TWO
ROPES OF EQUAL THICKNESS

## BOWLINE

USED FOR TYING ON
TO BELAY POINTS

## SLIP KNOT

GENERAL USE KNOT

## SHEEPSHANK

USED FOR SHORTENING

## SHEET BEND

FOR JOINING ROPES OF
UNEQUAL THICKNESS

## CLOVE HITCH

A NON SLIP KNOT

## SQUARE LASHING

......... CLOVE HITCH

10

# Knots Belays and Lashings.

The ability to be able to tie knots and safe sound lashings is a "must" for a survivor.

You never know when you will be required to use them to save your life. You may find that you are required to build yourself a raft of sorts so good knot lashing and belays are a must here. Even when you are building yourself a trap, or some form of shelter, once again a good knowledge of knots lashings and belays will stand you in good stead.

On the next page I have drawn a few of the most common ones. Each one has its own particular job.

As has been explained earlier one of the most important things for a good survivor is patience. Once you have got yourself organised into some form of camp discipline and everything running smoothly then you will probably find yourself with a little spare time. This is the ideal time for you to practise your knots and lashings and with a little practise you will be amazed just how quickly you can get yourself out of trouble by being able to tie knots correctly and quickly, for instance try trying a simple grannie knot with your hands under water especially water that is dark and muddy. Better still, try trying simple belay knots around yourself in the dark. It sounds simple enough but when your life may be depending on what you have just done then again you will be amazed how many times you re-check your knots.

Skills you can be taught, confidence you have to gain and you can only do this with a little time and effort. In other words 'practise makes perfect'.

## ROPES AND USES

### Knots and Lashes
### Tying up Rafts, Traps.

**FILTRATION**
WICKS FOR PETROL,
PARAFFIN, OILS, ETC.

**CANDLES**
DIPPED IN ANIMAL FATS,
OILS, ETC.

**WEAPONS**
BOWS, LASSOES, BINDINGS,
WHIPS

**FIRST AID**
SPLINTS, SLINGS,
BINDINGS, STRETCHERS.

**TRAPS**
BOXES, SNARES, LOOPS,
NETS, ETC.

**CLOTHING**
BELTS, BRACES, BINDINGS,
LACES.

**TRAPPING**
ANIMAL/MAN

**TYING UP**
ANIMAL, MAN, TRAPS, AIDS.

**FIRES**
SOAKING IN CHEMICALS,
ANIMAL FATS.

**CLIMBING**
RESCUE, ESCAPE, RECOVERY,
PROTECTION.

**SAFETY**
STRETCHER BINDINGS,
LOOPS, BRIDGES, SNARES,
NETS.

**TOWING**
BOATS, CARS, WOOD,
ANIMALS, RAFTS, ANIMALS,
ETC.

**WHIPS**
FISHING, WEAPONS,
ANIMAL CAGES.

**SIGNALS**
SLOW BURNING, CORDS FOR
TYING UP.

**FISHING**
TRAPS, NETS, LINES,
SNARES.

## Making Ropes from Bark, Grass, Cloth, Brambles.

Choose your bark well, Oak, for instance, unless properly treated, is not very good for rope making, whilst willow and other smooth barks are excellent.

## How to make Rope from Grass.

a.   Collect the longest grass you can find. Getting together two handfuls,

Soaking large lumps of bark

Soften by pulping on a stone or log

b.   Bend the grass over as per diagram, this prevents unwinding,

c.   Hold in right hand, twist the left strand (two turns) then push under the right. Continue now with the right strand, again twisting two turns and pushing under the left strand.

d.   To make the rope longer, just keep adding new grass when it is needed,

e.   If you are using cloth, first wet it. This will help you to make your twist much tighter, and stop it from springing loose.

Draw through spikes driven into a log

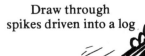

## Improvise a Lamp.

An excellent way of making a cheap lamp is to get the pith from either a marsh reed or elderberry.

Soak this well in animal fat and allow to dry out into straw sticks. Then stick the end into some soil or mud and light the other end and you will have a candle of sorts which will burn for a good 20 to 30 minutes.

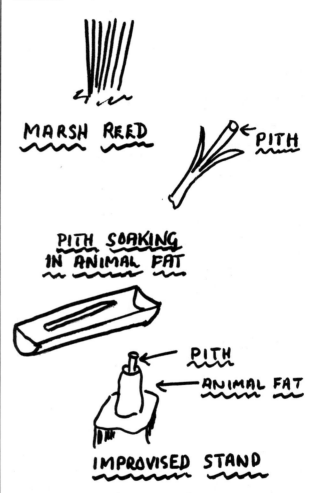

MARSH REED

PITH

PITH SOAKING IN ANIMAL FAT

PITH

ANIMAL FAT

IMPROVISED STAND

## Survival Needle.

Having learnt how to make fibres for cloth weaving either from animals or from plants then a must for the survivor is the survival needle. This can either be made from metal, wood, or bone.

If the needle is to be made from wood then it is important that the right type of wood is used and the best for this is any old hard wood. Some woods of course can be hardened by treating them. The best and simplest way is to bake the wood in the fire, or leave to dry out in the fire ashes.

Be you making the needle from wood, metal or bone then the making of them all is the same as in the diagrams. The principle is the same and the strength depends on what type of sewing you intend to do. For instance if you need to start sewing leather, especially leather that has not been treated correctly then you will find that the needle that you use needs to be extremely strong and supple. So, the best type I found for this kind of work was the bone one, and I found that the best types of bone to use were the splinters from the chicken legs once boiled and made as shown. Then I found that I had a first class needle to work with. Bone from the back of the fish I also found to be easy to work with.

All the diagrams are simple to follow, and self explanatory.

While working in the Middle East in the Muscat region I often used to sit and watch the local Arab girls sitting by the sea making needles from an assortment of fish bones. Some very small, some very large indeed. But in all cases they used to make them in the same way as I have described here.

Should the need arise for you to want a curved needle then this is not so difficult. Simply put the needle either into some hot water, or hold it over steam, and very quickly you will be able to make the shape you require. With wire of course you simply bend the shape that you need.

## Making a Candle from Animal Tallow Fats.

1. You will need something for the wick, a boot lace, a strip of bark or as above, (Marsh reed pith). Place the tallow into a container of boiling water and mix with bees wax. Boil, Scald and skim.
2. Now take the improvised wick, hang from a stick and dip into the tallow. Remove slowly and allow to dry. Repeat until desired thickness is reached.

## Making a Needle from Bone.

Select yourself a good piece of bone to work from. Preferably a chicken shin bone. These tend to splinter fine for this.

1. If possible try to get the bone shaped as shown in the diagram but the thick end needs to be about ¼ inch thick.

2. Now rub the needle on a stone until you have got it down to the thickness you need. Ensure that it is nice and thin and smooth (a little warm water here helps).

3. When you have got the bone to the thickness you require, find yourself a small pointed sharp stone (flint is excellent here).

FLINT HOLDER

FLINT

4. Place the needle on a flat surface (your polishing stone will do). Gently hold the needle in your left hand, and with the right hand holding the pointed stone very very carefully rub a small hole in the end of the needle to the size that you want.

5. All that remains now is to hold the needle on its side and very gently rub it down to the thickness you need, again on your polishing stone.

**Try This.** Here are a few simple hints for the use of the feather.

1. Firstly the feather float. Select yourself a good sized feather about 8" to 10" long.

BOTTOM                                                        TOP

2. Strip off all the feather fronds leaving yourself only the quill.

3. Working from the thin end (top) gently scrape or rub the quill until you have a very long tapered point.

TAPERED END

4. With a very fine sharp pointed stick pierce the quill about 2" from the top end piercing only half way into the quill.

← PIERCE HERE

5. Using warm water and a small round stick, roll the thin end of the feather to make it nice and supple.

6. When you have done this and got the end nice and supple, push it through the hole you made earlier in the quill. You should now end up with something like the one in the drawing shown.

7. You can if you wish tie up the end with hair from your head or as I have done many times, resin from the pine trees. This not only holds the end in, it also stops the water from getting into the float and waterlogging it.

← HUMAN HAIR
HORSE/ANIMAL HAIR

PINE RESIN

15

## Drop by Drop.

I have the armed services to thank for teaching me many things and one of them I am grateful for is the ability to jump from varying heights and be able to roll away successfully without hurting myself.

During my stay with airborne not only did I need this ability at the end of my parachuting but on many countless operational training exercises did it come in useful.

For myself I have no fear of heights, and this, coupled with the ability to roll correctly has possibly saved my life and certainly prevented serious injuries.

There is an art to this and to become proficient one must practise.

Dropping down from a wall for instance is not the same as dropping say from a tree branch. The ability for one to be able to twist and roll is a must. The ability for one to be able to absorb the shock throughout the body is also a must. For this there is no finer method than the parachute roll taught to the men of the airborne forces.

There is a limit of course to what height you can fall from and walk away from it safely. The highest that I have ever actually lowered myself over something and actually fallen was in fact twenty-eight feet. This I can promise you is a long way for someone to drop especially in the dark. People have been known to fall from greater heights than this, of course, and managed to get away safely.

You will see from the diagrams that the two techniques of dropping are different.

The first you will notice is that you must make an effort to turn away from the building on releasing. Otherwise you can finish up with your face smacking against the wall, and almost certainly you will damage your spine dropping this method if you have not been taught the correct procedure for falling.

The second is different altogether. This method is as near as damn it you can get to the actual parachute roll. Note the landing techniques on both the diagrams.

Surprise is a terrible thing especially if you are at the end of a rope lowering yourself down a cliff face or building. Suddenly the rope breaks and down you go. You need to be very quick indeed to be able to get yourself out of difficulty. So when lowering yourself down something always look down the rope or what have you. It is far better to have a bloody nose than a broken back or leg. I strongly recommend that you never attempt to climb down a rope two at a time. You need to be exceptionally strong in the arms to be able to hold someone in this method. The same goes for jumping from heights. I know that you often see people doing this on the films or television but remember they are more than probably professional stunt men and you can rest assured they never take unnecessary risks. They are true professionals always.

Of course I appreciate that the time may come when you may have to lower someone on the rope with you or jump into water, etc., but think before you do. Remember that it is better to have only one of you injured than two, for the sake of waiting another few minutes.

Old people of course no matter how much care we take always seem to hurt themselves when forced to drop from heights. So if you are caught in a situation where you may have to help out then you must think carefully and quickly. I can only say from my own experience that it is far better always to attempt to make some form of lowering aid no matter how rough than to expect say an old lady of sixty or seventy to jump. No amount of pushing will get her to go, unless she knows that there is something down there to catch her.

Jumping down forwards from great heights is not recommended nor indeed is dropping, unless you have learned to land correctly. To attempt either without training will almost certainly invite tragedy.

At one time when parachuting was in its infancy they used to teach this method but the casualty rate was so high that they had to find other methods very quickly. Hence the modern parachute roll, which is an excellent, safe method.

It is possible though to be able to land, get up and walk away from a fall in this fashion providing you follow the few simple safety rules and these are:

1. Always land on two feet (think of the young saplings and the old oak) landing on one leg is the sapling and landing on the two locked is the oak, and everyone knows which is the safer.

2. Keep your arms high and well forward, with the palms facing inwards. This reaching forwards action stops you from leaning your head back, and helps you to round your shoulders.

3. Always a flat footed landing. You are fighting for your safety not a gymnastic award.

4. And last but not least when you have completed your drop or fall then move away from the area quickly for if there are others behind you then you do not want them on the top of you.

Dropping from a bar or tree branch is another method altogether. Here it is vital that the person dropping must tuck the chin well into the chest, the shoulders well rounded, and the elbows brought well across the body. If this is not done then there is a very good chance that you may either break your arms by smashing your elbows on to the ground, break your nose or teeth by smashing your head down on to your knees on impact, or at the very worst, break your back by landing too rigidly on your legs.

There is what the parachutist call a forwards landing. This is when the body is being propelled forwards at a fast rate while falling. For this the parachutist is taught to turn his feet off at a given angle and on impact go into exactly the same method of rolling as shown, i.e. rolling down the side of the leg across the buttocks and finally the shoulders. It is well to remember that far more people hurt themselves when falling by sustaining what is best described as a head whip than by any broken bones, legs, arms etc. So chin in tight. If the person jumping is untrained, and there is any doubt about their landing then tie a sheet or towel or anything around their head to help as a buffer. You can mend a broken ankle or arm, but a neck?

AVOID DROPPING ON PROTRUDING ROOTS KEEP CHIN WELL TUCKED IN ELBOWS TUCKED ACROSS CHEST

AS WITH DROPPING FROM THE WALL HOLD THE TUCK AND ROLL FORWARDS PROTECTING THE HEAD AT ALL TIMES

LOOK DOWN AND ..OCK FEET HARD TOGETHER

Here you can see the method of dropping from a height from either the face of a building or from off a wall.

Note how the head is turned and one of the hands is used to push yourself clear from the wall surface. Note also how the landing is done and in particular the roll.

HEAD TURNED AND LOOKING DOWN

HAND PUSHING AWAY FROM WALL

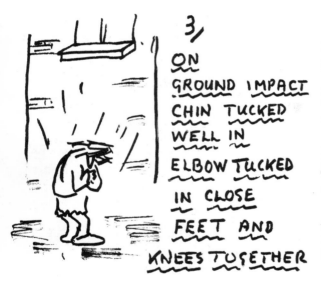

3/ ON GROUND IMPACT CHIN TUCKED WELL IN ELBOW TUCKED IN CLOSE FEET AND KNEES TOGETHER

In this method the techniques for lowering and landing are completely different. Here there is nothing for you to push from so positioning of the body for your landing is all important. You are more likely to hurt yourself dropping this method than the other one. This one I feel is the real back shaker.

As do the service men, practice jumping down from a chair or small box until you have managed to get some form of roll each time you land. You will be surprised at just how your confidence comes with a little practice.

The same landing techniques would be used if you were dropping from the end of a rope, the only difference being that you would have to twist your feet away from the rope, when you release.

4/ IMMEDIATELY ON IMPACT PUSH THE SIDE OF YOUR LEG OUT. KEEP ELBOWS WELL TUCKED IN

5/ CONTINUE ROLL KEEPING LEGS AND FEET LOCKED HARD TOGETHER

# Try These
## Common Puff Ball & Cobweb
(Lycoperdon Perlatum) Edible

Found peaty ground/meadows/coniferous woods (European countries) especially around birches.

Season — July to late September.

Nutrition value. Very little. Must be eaten when fresh. Gives good taste to soups.

### Preparation

Collect fresh puff balls and you will find that they are beautiful and white inside.

At this stage they are edible and ready for eating. Prepare them as normal mushrooms though you gain no nutritional value from their stalks.

DICE

It is the puff ball that has gone through the eating stage that we want. When broken open, you will find instead of the beautiful white flesh a dark brown powder, so that when you pierce the ball the powder squirts out.

We have a use for this powder which is a form of penicillin. Using cobweb and water it becomes part of our first aid kit.

COB WEB

5. If you have a cut say on your wrist that's not too deep, place some of the cobwebs over it, sprinkle with hot water to make them form to the shape of the cut. Next, sprinkle some of the puff ball spores on to the cobweb.

6. What happens is the cobwebs form a kind of natural fibrinigen over the cut giving a better healing power helped by the crude penicillin.

---

## "Firewood"

Sometimes the fuel for the fire that we need urgently is not always available (mainly wood) so the survivor must turn again to improvisation skills.

Remember the rule for cooking. You need good hot embers to cook well, so your substitute fuels must, where possible, provide them.

Grass, for instance, is of no use at all in the making of embers but used correctly on a fire can help the survivor in many ways. For instance, wet grass makes heavy white smoke, useful for signalling on moors or jungle terrain, while the ash from the grass makes excellent filtration powder for water purification and indeed poultices.

Grass used in improvising peat blocks also works very well. To make these blocks you will need fresh animal dung (the wetter the better) some green damp grass, a few twigs and, of course, a fire or hot embers.

This method of making fuel for burning is still very widely used abroad even today, especially by desert people.

The making process may sound offensive and possibly crude, but I can assure you the end product is well worth it.

Making a few blocks is simple. Mix the fresh dung with the grass into a round ball. Ensure that it is well and truly mixed and in this European climate you would have to place the ball near to a fire to dry out effectively, but in the desert regions then placing the ball on a hot stone in the sun will do just as well.

Once dried out then the fuel can be stored ready for use as any ordinary peat block would be.

Mix as before, place over hot embers, stick some of the twigs through as shown on the diagram. When you see the block drying out remove by the sticks.

Just before you go to sleep at night, place one of these on the fire and you will be surprised and amazed at the amount of time it takes for one reasonably sized block to burn through.

## Wild Honey

Did you know that a wild bee honeycomb melted down makes an excellent throat healer, and that you can cook most of your meals in the oils melted down from the combs? Bees wax, rubbed on your fishing line, prevents it from sinking or the same wax rubbed into your boots helps make them water-proof and helps prevent the leather from cracking. And did you know that by rubbing bees wax on your hands before setting traps helps to hide your scent?

One of the best natural fishing baits you can get is honey, sprinkled on the water around your fishing float it will gently float down to the bottom, but in so doing, it starts to break up into small pieces. The fish begin to nibble and get the taste. Soon they begin to start grabbing at the best of the honey and become really greedy.

I know of one old lady who uses nothing else but honey melted down for her poultices, and of course every one knows that honey in tea is a real sweetener, especially if the tea has been made from wild herbs, and is probably a little bitter.

## Making Butter.

Making butter in the wilds is not as difficult as one would think. Any kind of milk will do: Cow Goat or Sheep.

Use only fresh milk if possible; skim the top of the milk daily. Milk left to stand for an hour or so will settle and give you a skim of cream each time. Try to keep the cream cool while it is being stored. And every time you collect fresh cream, mix it thoroughly with the other as soon as you possibly can. Once you have done this, leave the cream mix to stand for about twenty four hours or so, still keeping the contents nice and cool, if possible between twelve and twenty degrees centigrade. Especially so in warm weather. It is not necessary to have a churn to mix the butter. Any small waterproof container will do at this stage. Mix thoroughly for about twenty to thirty minutes until the mix starts to turn yellow. These of course are the globules of your butter. When you have got together all the butter you think you are going to get from this mix, pour the contents into a strainer of sorts. This will separate the now made butter from the remaining mix. While the butter is at this stage it is a good idea to wash it to remove all the remaining milk. Once you have done this, using a flat board surface and mixing paddle, bring together all the butter globules to form your butter cob. This is pure and simple survival butter. Some people I know when making butter this way before they make the butter cob give the butter globules a wash in water about the same temperature as the butter itself. This again washes away any excess milk that may have been left and as they quite rightly say, makes the butter clean and pure.

## Psychological "Warfare"

A friend of mine in the Army once told me about the time he had been in the far east as a prisoner during the last war.

He said that one of the main reasons for the cause of so many deaths amongst the soldiers had been the lack of proper food and medicines, and of course the lack of these did not help the medical staff's image in not being able to combat the growing dysentry rate that was rife out there. The medical officers in charge there were at their wit's end trying to cure the sick, both in sickness and morale.

One particular medical officer there came up with a brilliant scheme to help combat this however.

Here is how my friend told it to me.

One day the M.O. was feeling really low himself at not being able to help his men recover from this terrible disease because of the lack of the drugs needed to cure them. But he knew that if he could help build up the men's morale a little higher then this in itself would be a help.

So one day he sent his orderly out into the jungle to collect some bamboo shoots and stems, whilst he himself set about collecting some of the many jungle berries known to him that abounded around the camp. Once these were collected together, he mixed the berries and some acquired chalk with water and the bamboo shoots, mixing all of these together to make a gooey off-red chalky paste, he then proceeded to take out the pith from the bamboo that the orderly had brought back. He knew that once boiled the bamboo shoots would soon harden again if left out for a few days in the sun, so he poured the concoction into the hollowed-out bamboo and put them out to dry. Once this was done he set about telling everyone in the camp that a new supply of drugs had got through and would be here in a couple of days. This of course had just the effect on the men's morale that he wanted. Already some of the men's morale began to rise. For two days he kept the supply story going thus easing the story that he would have to make up explaining just how he had suddenly acquired a fresh supply of new drugs. Things went fine and about two days later he began to remove the now dried mixture from his bamboo mould and started to cut them up into small pills and tablets. As quickly as he did this his orderly began to put the home made drugs into the already empty bottles and boxes on his shelves. He also made up various concoctions of coloured berry juices to supplement his medicine supplies that had long ago diminished. Two days later and now fully armed again so to speak he waited for the usual sick paraders in the morning. Some were genuine while many others were just plain malingerers. Morning came and the sick parade with it. He showed them his newly acquired medical supplies and began supplying new medicines and drugs (though he knew himself that medicinally they could have no effect at all but psychologically they might help). Next he sat back and waited, wondering what the response from the men would be. Well, he need not have worried at all, the response was terrific. So many of the familiar malingerers soon drifted back to work that he thought that he had found a new wonder drug. But what my friend told me in fact did happen was that the men whom the doctor treated said afterwards "Bugger going to see that quack of a doctor, all he gives you is a lump of soggy coloured chalk and some weak looking coloured water; it is safer to go out on the bloody chain gang than to go to him for treatment".

A good story? Well my source of information is pretty reasonable and I do not doubt him.

## Methods of Crossing a River.

Be you crossing alone or in a party, either way extra special care must be taken at all times.

No matter how you try it is practically impossible to be able to judge with any accuracy just how strong or deep a river is when you come across one in the wilds. A would-be survivor has found himself literally in deep water by not following simple safety rules.

One golden rule of any river crossing is always try to cross as near the start of the source as possible. Here the water may not be so deep and quite possibly the stream will not be so wide. Another important factor here is that in the early stages the stream will not have very steep banks which in themselves present to the survivor a hazard. These I know are simple things but even so are often forgotten.

It is not always possible I know for the survivor to get to the source of the river. He may have joined it too far down to go all the way back up-stream to cross. However the effort involved in even attempting is a must even if you only go a few hundred yards or so.

Rivers of course are one of the world's main supply routes and to the survivor are in fact a life saver. Should you find yourself (after wandering around for a few days) lucky enough to have stumbled on one then stay with it. From it you can start planning your rescue. All animal life at one time or other will come to the river to feed. In foreign countries the locals all use the river for transport and in some cases for habitation. In the event of a rescue being operated the pilots will use the rivers as marker boundaries.

Food and vegetation all grow on the river bank so your chances of survival are so much greater. While you are resting and recuperating, you can also start to plan how you intend to cross the river you need to.

Look at the diagrams and they will show you some of the recommended ways for a group to cross.

I am often asked why do I emphasise that the person who is crossing the stream always force up-stream. Well there are one or two good points for this method and they are:

When one walks facing up-stream the water pressure on the front of the legs keeps the legs straight and stops them from giving way under strong force whilst if the survivor were facing down-stream possibly the water would force him to bend at the knees, and should you have a weight on your shoulders at the time this could prove to be dangerous indeed. By facing up-stream you are also alert to anything that may be floating down towards you that could possibly be dangerous to you. Remember if you do use a rod to assist you in crossing you must be exceptionally careful that the water force does not wash the rod under your feet and cause you to trip over. Move slowly and deliberately. If you have waited that long before crossing then you can afford to take your time in crossing, and as I have said earlier if you have a large pack on your back then take extra special care. I always remove one of the shoulder straps from my shoulder (the one on the shoulder away from the river force as shown in the diagram)

Always when crossing on your own, if you have to, walk slightly up-stream again as shown. Many would-be survivor has found himself in difficulty by removing the wrong shoulder strap, and by walking down-stream and most important of all facing the wrong way i.e. down-stream.

If you do walk down-stream the wrong way then the force of the water behind your legs can quite easily make you buckle at the knees and if you have not removed one of your shoulder straps then you can imagine what kind of trouble you can get into.

Sometimes it may not be possible for you to cross the river by fording. You may find you might have to build yourself some form of a bridge if you are that determined to cross the river. Well if the bridging materials are handy and you are fit enough and have the time then why not. But remember this. Once you have left the safety of the bank then you are on your own and if your bridge has not been constructed correctly then you are in for trouble.

However, do not let this deter you if you are so determined. Like everything else go about it methodically, think things out and build safely.

When building consider the weather and its very rapid changes, especially if you are in an area that is susceptible to rapid river flooding. Consider the materials that you want to build the bridge with. I remember on one jungle trip I made, the wood that we intended to use was in fact far too heavy for us to carry to the river bank and when we did eventually get the log to the water it was nowhere near long enough for the job. Once again simple things but at the time were forgotten.

Learn to judge the width and depth of the river. A couple of tried and tested ways that one can use are shown in the diagrams. It is also possible for one to be able to judge the speed of flow when building the bridge. Always have a good look down the stream for any danger points that you may find yourself in, should anything happen to you on the crossing. For example, waterfalls, hidden tree branches, sharp rocks. Remember if you find your bridge washed away while you are on it, then it is impossible for you to steer the thing. For you to get any steering at all then the raft or broken bridge that you are standing on must be travelling faster than the water surface. Without this you are at the mercy of the water force. So think very deeply before you attempt to make yourself some form of improvised bridge at all. Having said this of course the need may arise when you have to build yourself something. If it is for a simple crossing then there will be no need for you to attempt to build a massive big thing that is going to take a long time and a lot of your very much needed strength.

It is possible with a little ingenuity to build a strong but simple bridge capable of crossing a river of over twenty feet wide.

Never be tempted to use wood that has been lying around for a long time on the floor. It may be well rotted and as soon as you attempt to put any weight on it, it will more than probably break up.

## Improvised Swimming Aids.

Even in this modern age there are still thousands of people who cannot swim, and it's tragic when you think, and consider that two thirds of the Earth's surface is water.

It's surprising how many methods the survivor will come up with when under pressure.

Tins, bottles, logs, old cans, plastic bags, boxes; the list is endless. Improvisation is the key word here for the survivor. The diagrams show only a few simple but effective ways of aiding the non-swimmer. These of course are mainly for the deep water survivor.

RUCKSAC OFF THE SHOULDER

One very important rule whenever you ar crossing any stretch of water (be it deep or shallow that you feel is not deep enough to swim is alway carry a stick for probing before entering the water

Never, never, never dive or jump into water tha you think may have hidden dangers. Always, wher possible, enter the water feet first, and by lowerin yourself into it gradually.

24

# Improvised Swimming Aids.

1.   Remove your trousers/skirt. Tie up the leg ends securely. Button/zip the fly, hold the waist band (zip/fly nearest your shoulder). Then when you do jump into the water swing the trousers over your head and pull down hard under the water.

At this stage you will find that the trousers will have inflated, and all that you do now is to manoeuvre yourself between the inflated trouser legs and support your body weight.

It is better if you soak the trousers first before actually jumping.

This is an excellent method and gives good support, and with a little practice and improvisation other parts of the clothing could be improvised just as easily.

It is possible for the survivor to re-inflate the trousers even though he may still be in the water.

It is possible to keep the trousers inflated for a good half an hour.

## Crossing a Stream or Ravine.

A safe and tried method of placing two logs across a gap be it stream or ravine to make a simple foot bridge is shown in the diagrams below.

Once you have determined the width of the gap and you are fortunate enough to be in an area where there are stout logs to use for a bridge then all that's required is for you to cut down a couple of desired lengths.

The diagrams will best explain for you the simple way of manipulating the logs into the required position.

1. A. Log length     b. Gap width

2. First log in position

3. Second log in position

4. Logs across and secured

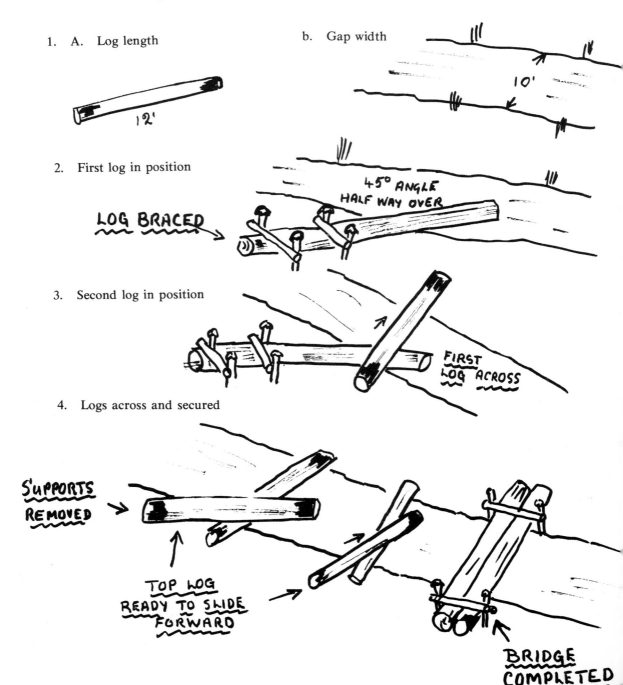

26

## Measuring the Width of a River or Ravine.

If you have no compass and you need to measure the width of a stream or river to cross, then perhaps the following will help you:

Take a sighting on a prominent object, say a tree. Place a stick or a stone as near as you can square to it (see diagram), and measure. Set up your second marker forming as near a right angle as you can (see diagram).

Repeat this angle on your side of the bank until lines 'A', 'B' and 'C' run true. This will give you the width of the river to within 6" or so.

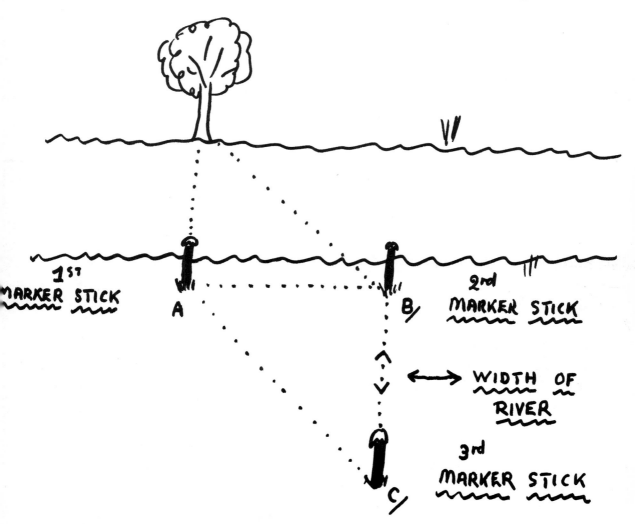

1ˢᵀ MARKER STICK

A

2ⁿᵈ MARKER STICK

B

← → WIDTH OF RIVER

3ʳᵈ MARKER STICK

C

# 2 Tracking and Direction

## Walking in different Terrains.

There are people who specialise in walking moorlands, forests, and old cart tracks, while others enjoy the thrill of walking deserts, and even tropical jungles, and each one requires its own expertise in method and equipment.

For instance, it is impossible to travel as fast in the jungle, especially secondary jungle (that is jungle that has overgrown with thick scrub and bush after the trees have either been cleared by burning and timber removed), as for instance, over hard open moorland, though we all know that certain areas of moorland can be treacherous and boggy as well. Any one who has travelled for long distances over soft sand will know equally as well just how hard on the feet and tiring on the legs this can be.

Each terrain has its own peculiarities. For example, weather changes, especially on the moors. Intense heat during the day quickly changing to extreme cold at night in the desert, while in the jungle a continual feeling of being closed in coupled with very humid conditions both day and night. On the open hills one tends to get a false sense of security and safety especially if the day is beautifully clear and with a clear blue sky. In the desert because there are very few landmarks and tracks or roads then a very different sense of security comes over you, and you find yourself wondering if you are going in the right direction or not, you are continually checking your direction. And as for walking in the jungle, unless you are actually walking on a track or known route, then it is practically impossible to find your true direction unless you are either an experienced jungle walker or you have the correct navigation aids, such as compass, maps etc.

Let's take for instance the moorlands and mountains in Great Britain. Walking moorland and climbing mountains are two very different things, and must not in any way be confused with each other. We are lucky in this country that we have governing bodies who go to great lengths to ensure our safety and protection by providing proper equipment, marked routes, proper instructional courses, and the world's best air, sea, and mountain rescue services.

## Walking in Different Terrains and Conditions.

Hill or moorland walking in Great Britain is practically a national sport, and certainly one of the most popular pursuits in this country and indeed in countries like Germany, Austria, Sweden and other countries that have miles of rolling moorlands, hills and beautiful forest covered mountains.

However, like all good things there are always some people who are not satisfied with just going out and enjoying the beautiful sights and areas that nature has so graciously provided for us. Man being what he is always wants to strive further forward and test new unexplored territory. I don't think there is a year goes by in this country that we don't hear about someone being lost or killed even in the hills and moors here in Britain, and yet, if the people concerned only followed the simple but tried and tested rules that help towards our safety, then half of the accidents need never happen at all.

Everyone knows that accidents do happen and that in many cases they can be avoided if proper precautions are carried out. Always ensure that if you intend to go mountain climbing for instance you have the proper equipment needed to ensure your safety, and let other people know when, where, and how you intend to travel.

Now you may think that all this is getting away from pure survival. Well the answer to this is, in the first place, no matter what indoor or outdoor activity you intend to do, always try to get some information on it.

I never, ever attempt to go out into the wild anywhere in the world without making some effort to find out a few local points. One of the things they taught me in the army is always try to get local information and experience. This is invaluable and time-saving and in some sad cases life-saving.

Every time I travel, be it by air or sea, I always make a point of keeping a mental note of the direction, time, and the date. In each case it only takes a couple of seconds but it is well worth the effort, and as I have explained already, a simple survival kit is not too difficult to make and carry with you. Like the fire is to the Boy Scout, I feel the presence of that small but invaluable survival kit in my pocket is a terrific morale booster, and the knowledge of what it will help me to do in cases of emergency helps my confidence.

Each one of the different terrains and the countries continually keep offering up to you, the survivor, way of testing your skills like safety aids, patience and over all power to stay alive. Any sailor will tell you treat the sea with respect and you will reap its rewards, slacken for a moment and it will have you. This rule can be said for all the other terrains as well. If you're working on land, take a tip from nature, take things easy where you need to, watch the wild life how it survives, moves, and indeed eats. Keep a continual look out and a wary eye on the weather. We may be able to put a man on the Moon, and bring him back safely but there is one thing than man has not yet learnt to do and that is to control the weather, or indeed forecast it accurately. Yet, the funny thing is, some wild animals can do a far better assessment of climatic changes than any modern machine or man's guess. Having said this I think it is only fair to say that there are some types of men in some of the wilder unexplored parts of the world who in fact can give very accurate readings of the weather indeed. The North American Indian for instance was very knowledgable on the subject, and the Australian Aborigine I found to be superb and very accurate almost to the hour with their weather reading. And yet I have known so-called professional explorers who with all their claimed widely travelled experience just push aside any advice offered up to them. These people are a danger to themselves and in lots of cases to others by either bad leadership, lack of control, and in most cases lack of genuine experience, and common sense.

The British Mountain Climbing Association, and the Rambling Society are without doubt two of the many excellent societies that one can get accurate and updated information from that only boost your knowledge and confidence if you intend to either plan an expedition or just go off and walk alone.

There are some who would say that it is wrong for one person to go off walking alone. Well I personally think that this is not so. That is if the person who wants to go it alone remembers the simple survival rules that one needs to know if travelling alone. I myself am very much a loner, and when I do travel alone I always ensure that I have taken the necessary precautions for my safety.

I can not stress too strongly just how important it is to ensure that you take all the necessary precautions that you must take to aid your safety and comfort when undertaking any adventure that has a strong element of danger.

As well as giving excellent advice on the conditions and the routes etc, etc, the Mountain Society and Ramblers and the other many excellent associations that we have, also give out recommendations on the best type of clothing and equipment to use. These people have had years of very valuable and practical experience so do listen and take heed.

I remember on one expedition a friend of mine offered to make me a route map of the area that I was going into on a silk handkerchief giving all the local, and updated information. I of course jumped at this and had one made for me; needless to say all the time I was on the expedition I had to continually keep my eyes on it as the others in the party soon realised just how invaluable it was. But the point I am trying to get across to you is that a small piece of silk handkerchief like this which weighed nothing at all gave me a tremendous feeling of safety and knowledge.

I can't mention the number of times that I have come through the customs, and the customs officers have smiled at me when they saw my assortments of goodies laid out in front of them; especially things like my snares, improvised knives, fishing gear, etc. And one particular customs officer became so engrossed in my bits and pieces and where and what I had been doing that he actually came on one of my courses himself for the sole purpose of going off with some of his friends and trying his new found skills out.

However once again I say to you, do make the effort to ensure your safety if you intend to go off alone. Ask around. You will be surprised just how much information you can acquire, and how helpful people can be.

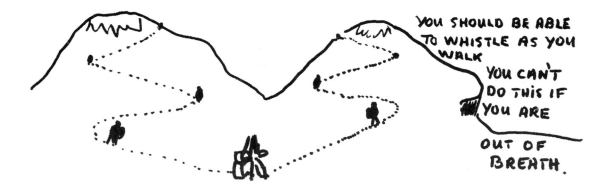

YOU SHOULD BE ABLE TO WHISTLE AS YOU WALK

YOU CAN'T DO THIS IF YOU ARE

OUT OF BREATH.

## Moorland and Mountain Terrain

Moorland and mountain terrain present problems of extreme cold and winds, and these of course can and do lead to exposure.

Because the moorlands are so exposed temperatures can change so very quickly; this is because there is nothing to act as buffers, or stops for the very cold strong winds that do occur, and because of the varying heights of the hills so dramatic temperature changes also occur. Every school boy knows that on clear cloudless nights the temperature drops considerably. And when the sky is covered with cloud then the night is so much warmer. But it is surprising how many of the children I have spoken to on my lectures think that the temperature on top of a mountain is the same as that down in the valley. And though I hate to admit it so do many grown ups. There are many who certainly think that because the mountain is covered in cloud that the temperature is much warmer than an uncovered one and this of course is perfectly true but what they have not taken into consideration is the height and geographical location of the mountain.

An interesting set of figures given to me by a gentleman who was on a television interview with me a few years ago was that for every one person either lost or killed in the jungle or the desert, nearly fifty anually are lost or injured in either the mountains or moorlands right here in Britain, and in nearly every case the mountain rescue people claim that inadequate training was not done before setting off, and that the proper clothing needed to ensure safety was not used.

At the rear of the book I have listed a number of first class books that one can purchase from most book shops that will give you all the many excellent tips and practical advice that you might need. It is not my intention in this book to list all the many varied clothing and equipment one can buy.

Walking on steep-sided ground requires a skill of its own.

Anyone who has tried to climb steeply upwards in a straight line on a wet slippery mountainside will know just how difficult this can be. In fact if the hill is too steep then it is nearly impossible.

There is a good technique for walking on steep ground and if a few simple rules are followed then a lot of wasted effort can be avoided.

One has only to look at the shepherds who daily have to move up and down the mountains and hills and see the methods they use. In fact it's funny really when you see the shepherd walking along in a nice quiet methodical way, and a couple of amateur hikers scrambling along trying to get to the summit as quickly as possible, ten minutes before the shepherd who arrives fresh, fit and still moving whilst they are invariably sitting gasping for breath.

It is very rare that you see any animal life bounding directly upwards. Nearly always you see them zig-zagging across a slope as the shepherd does.

If you are carrying a pack of equipment on your back then walking directly upwards is not only impossible (for long distances) but downright dangerous.

By the zig-zag method at least you get a chance to ease off the unnecessary aches and pains that are caused by continually walking on one particular part of the foot and if you are traversing ice belts then from the lateral position you can dig in more easily with your ankles/inside foot or ice-pick if you have one available.

I personally never walk the hill unless I have a stout walking stick or rod with me for balance, and for control I find it invaluable.

Another thing about traversing the hill is that one may cover a little more ground but from the air rescuers have a far better chance of spotting you because of your irregular movement pattern.

## Jungle Aids.

Bamboo grows all over the world, not necessarily in jungles. It is not uncommon to find large bamboos growing in English gardens and parks. Bamboo is useful for making tools, and traps, and can also serve as a food source. Bamboo shoots are well known in the West through Chinese restaurants, and the leaves after boiling are edible too.

At the base of the larger green bamboo is a white turnip-tasting area, which can be boiled for food when the bark has been removed.

Even the roots, once you have managed to dig them out, can be boiled for eating, but they need to be cooked three times and the water thrown away each time to get rid of the earthy taste.

HOLLOWED OUT SECTION USED FOR COOKING

BOTTOM OF GREEN BAMBOO USED FOR EATING ONCE OUTER CORE AS BEEN REMOVED

## Uses of Peat.

As many people know, large areas of Ireland are covered in peat, and for centuries it has been used for burning. As a survivor you can easily make use of this method. Peat contains large quantities of water which needs to be driven off before using. To dry it thoroughly, once you have cut it from the ground in useful blocks, put it on a rack, as shown in the diagrams. Dried, it contains about 60% carbon and 32% oxygen, with a small percentage of hydrogen. Oils, tar and ammonia can also be extracted from it.

Peat forming as the mosses edge out from the banks of a small lake, some dead and decaying matter sinking to the bottom.

Once the lake has been taken over completely a swamp begins to form.

After a while the swamp tends to dry up a little and in some parts of the world it is encouraged by the locals in the way of drainage. This is to make it safe and workable for cutting and removal.

Stacking is most important at this stage to help dry out the peat, and once dried it is now ready for burning or for breaking down into compost.

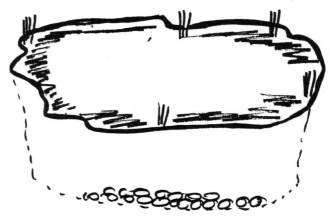

MOSS FORMING ON THE LAKE EDGE

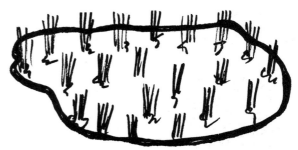

LAKE COMPLETELY COVERED IN MOSS

DIGGING PEAT OUT

PEAT DRYING ON RACKS

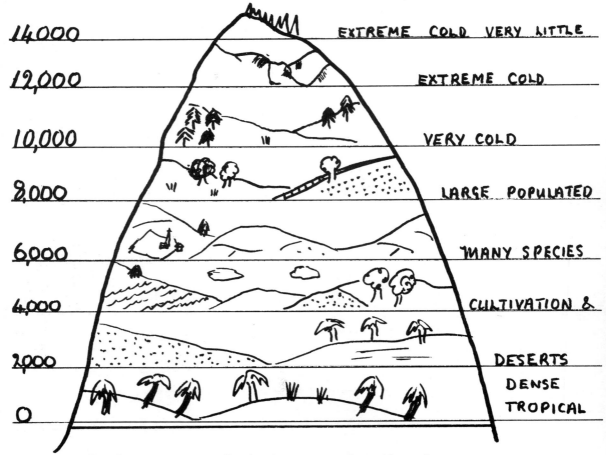

14000 — EXTREME COLD VERY LITTLE

12,000 — EXTREME COLD

10,000 — VERY COLD

8,000 — LARGE POPULATED

6,000 — MANY SPECIES

4,000 — CULTIVATION &

2,000 — DESERTS

0 — DENSE TROPICAL

A SKETCH VIEW SHOWING HOW
THE ZONES CHANGE MOVING UP A
MOUNTAIN SLOPE.

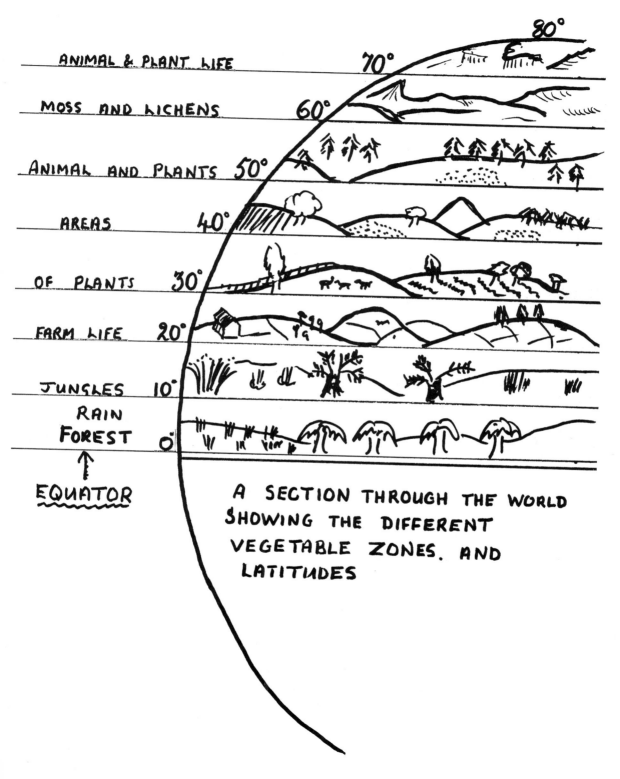

ANIMAL & PLANT LIFE 70° 80°

MOSS AND LICHENS 60°

ANIMAL AND PLANTS 50°

AREAS 40°

OF PLANTS 30°

FARM LIFE 20°

JUNGLES 10°

RAIN FOREST 0°

↑
EQUATOR

A SECTION THROUGH THE WORLD
SHOWING THE DIFFERENT
VEGETABLE ZONES. AND
LATITUDES

# EXAMPLES OF HOMES IN USE THROUGHOUT
# THE WORLD

GUATEMALAN
THATCHED HOUSE

NORTH AMERICAN
TEPEE

ESKIMO IGLOO
WINTER

AUSTRALIAN LEAF
HOUSE

SKINS

ESKIMO SUMMER
HOUSE

SOUTH AMERICAN LEAF
HOUSE

DESERT
SANGER

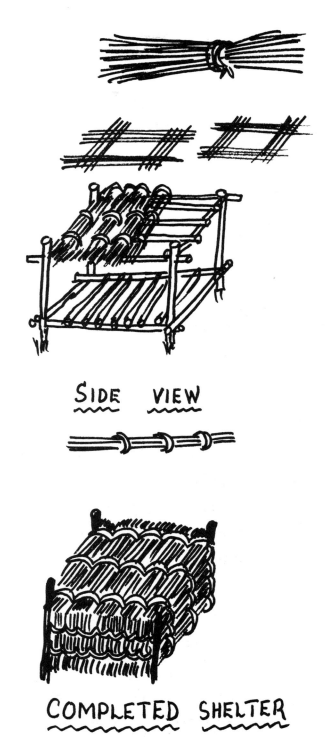

## Waterproofing Your Shelter.

Gather together enough small 9" thin supple twigs to bind your thatchings together.

Collect together a large quantity of the materials you want to thatch with, in this case we will use grass or reeds.

Ensure that it is all lying the same way, then separate it into small but workable bunches.

Once again lay it on the lattice work, starting from the bottom upwards.

As you lay so you must pin each piece with your small thatching twigs.

As with the leaves, overlap and each one needs individual pinning. Work your way up to the top row.

When you reach the apex of your shelter you need to start bending over the thatchings pinning from underneath and above.

This method of thatching is very old, well tried and tested and very simple to do, and with a little practice and patience you will soon become very proficient at it.

SIDE VIEW

THATCHING TWIGS

COMPLETED SHELTER

SIDE VIEW

HOO

## Waterproofing Your Shelter.

If you are using natural material such as grass, leaves, branches, ferns etc. then this page will guide you simply through your choice.

1. The use of leaves. First you must build your framework as shown in the diagram.
2. Gather the largest leaves you can find but you must ensure that they are fresh.
3. Now gently cut a hook in the stem as shown. Place these over the bottom lat working along the bottom first, as a professional tiler would.
4. Overlapping is a must here if you intend to stay in the shelter more than a couple of nights.

The same system can also be used for sealing the sides. Remember the bigger the shelter the more you will require to cover, and the more materials you will need to collect to build.

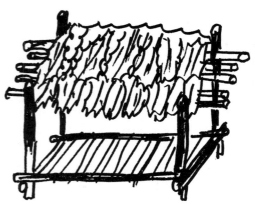

A TYPICAL THATCHED LEAF SHELTER

## Basic Survival Tracking.

The history of survival tracking is as old as man himself.

When he developed a taste for meat, he met new problems. Vegetables never ran or fought back. They were easy to get and in abundance, but unfortunately they were seasonal. This posed a problem for him during the winter months so he had to find a food substitute.

He must have quickly learned that his source of meat was very dangerous, and cunning and even though it was often bigger, faster and more ferocious than himself, he could in fact outwit and out-think it. In order to do this and survive man developed his tracking and trapping techniques, and as he developed even further he found these skills could be helpful for a variety of other reasons.
1. Food sources.
2. Guarding against enemy attack.
3. The capture of slaves.
4. Greed, revenge, lust, jealousy.
5. To gather information.
6. To provide working animals etc.

## Visual Tracking.

### HOT AND DRY

Signs are difficult and dusty especially if there is any wind although dust can often aid the trained tracker. Game is often lethargic, and young game becomes carefree and careless. Foliage is brittle and easily broken. Noise carries long distances.

### COLD

Snow forest: game is scarce due to some hibernation. Food is scarce for both man and animals, but tracking is much easier.

To assist you in your tracking, try to break up the signs into three groups. (These groups signs can also be caused by the tracker himself, so beware!).

**TOP SIGNS** From shoulder upwards.
**MIDDLE SIGNS** Between shoulders and knees.
**BOTTOM SIGNS** Knees to ground.

Below are a few examples of these signs.

**TOP SIGNS** Birds fluttering from branches are a definite warning to the animals below that an enemy is approaching, strands of human hair left on twigs etc.

**MIDDLE SIGNS** Branches pushed aside by man or large animals, human body scent, broken twigs or bruises on trees caused by dragging kit etc.

**BOTTOM SIGNS** Tracks, urine, and droppings, snapped twigs, bruises, holes, etc. Insects rising and animals scurry across the ground, burrows, spit, waste droppings, discarded fur, vomit, old food droppings, rain puddles, unbroken plants.

Note: bird droppings, once identified can be found in all tree areas, and can relate to tree nesting birds, or game birds who spend a lot of their time on the ground.

Practise your tracking whenever possible, it could save your life sometime.

### HELPFUL NOTES

Generally speaking plants in their natural state tend to look one way only; towards the light and sun.

Animals tend to look two ways; forwards and down.

Man tends to look five ways; downwards, upwards, forwards and sideways.

With training man also looks inwards (deep thinking and concentration).

It helps when tracking to practise a little mental telepathy. Try throwing an emotion at someone sitting a short distance away from you.

Try calling their name inwardly.

Try calling the game you are stalking.

Try reading his or their minds.

Try to get them or it to run and look at you.

# REMEMBER MAN CAN'T FLY

## Visual Tracking Skills

With tracking, you cannot bluff, you either know where you are going or you don't. It is useless to pretend that you are following a good set of signs when you know in your heart that the signs mean nothing.

When I was in the army they used to have a simple but effective rule: If in doubt, step out. What they meant here is, if you found that you were completely lost then stop and either rest or let someone else take over, remembering that tracking in the army generally meant that you were in 'Live' country and more often than not you were leading others behind you and this probably meant into an enemy ambush area.

The art of tracking people or animals over different types of terrain is not only very skilful and requires lots of patience and a skilful eye, but it is very rewarding when you come up with the right results. With regular practice you are not only able to follow signs effectively but you will be able to tell whether the signs are male or female, young or old, injured, sick or fit and even carrying something or indeed someone. It is also possible to tell whether the person you are tracking is indeed trying to out-wit you. Remember it is impossible for man to move across any ground without leaving some form of sign. Man cannot fly, so unless he is using some form of aid to cross the ground, then it is impossible for him not to leave a sign of some sort.

Things that help the tracker are our age, sex, fitness and more often than not, cunning.

Normally when man walks he walks in what I call the 'heel toe pyramid' style. By this I mean the man's normal natural gait. In this he tends to put down his heel first making a very definite imprint, then rolling onto his toe this being hardly visible as the man moves from foot to foot. At this stage he is transferring his weight evenly and regularly. This to the tracker tells him that the person he is tracking is fit, fresh and seems to have no worries or indeed any intimation that he is being followed in any way. Should the man's signs suddenly change into a more definite toe sign with the forward edge of the toe showing a good clean edge then this tells the tracker that the person he is tracking has now changed into a hard, fast, running action and is still fresh in body and stamina and has possibly now suspected that he is being followed. Should the toe sign suddenly start to spurt sand/soil backwards then the person is trying to run as fast as he possibly can and in so doing, he is unknowingly helping his tracker. To out-wit your tracker effectively, try to remain as normal and as fresh as possible. Running on the side of your feet or trying to run backwards or any other way, to out-wit him, only helps him. For instance, trying to run on the outside of your feet tells the tracker that you are conscious of him being near, that you have shortened your stride and that you are now trying to beat him at his own game. This is fine, but remember, he has all the time in the world to find you, while you are the one who needs to put as much space between you as you can.

40

## Tracking

What I've tried to do here is to simplify how different signs tell the tracker what he wants to know.

When I started to learn tracking I was always taught to try to listen with my eyes and look with my ears. This is not as silly as it seems. All five senses come into your tracking but sometimes you need to try to cross them a little to help you out. An example is, try watching someone some distance off but not only watching, listening to his footsteps even though it is impossible for you to hear him from where you are. What you start to do unconsciously is to put yourself in the place of the person you are watching and before long, you find that you are indeed crossing two of your senses without knowing it. This is exactly what happens to you when tracking someone or thing you cannot see, or has gone past a few hours before. Each sign no matter how little should give you a picture and a sound relation. Another good tip is to stop now and then especially if you think that the person or thing you are following knows they are being followed. This is when your mental telepathy comes in handy — you will be surprised how close to the real thing you can come by using this method. Again you unconsciously start putting yourself into the position of the person who is being tracked, and a peculiar thing about mental telepathy is when your minds do cross, generally the person being tracked tries to out-wit you by changing either his route, his body action and indeed his mental approach, so when you come along the track to the place where your minds crossed you will invariably find the tell-tale marks telling you.

This of course needs lots of practise and indeed confidence. Some trackers are very good, while others only bluff. The aborigines are exceptionally good at the mental telepathy. While in Africa, I found the pygmies working mostly on signs only.

## Visual Tracking Tell-tales

It is not commonly known that everyone's foot, like the handshake, are individual tell-tale signs.

Each foot varies just a little and has a definite character sign just like the finger prints of the hand.

Once when working in the Oman I had the good fortune to be able to work with a scout from the Sudan. This man had been employed by the Arab government to act as a tracker.

I used to make a point of going out with this man whenever the chance arose. His powers of observation were fantastic, he never wore shoes at all and his ability to track in the night was just as keen if not keener, than in the day time.

Once when we were tracking the adu (enemy) I remember him stopping by a small stone on the ground and actually smelling the stone, then standing up and moving forward a few paces he would turn around, and try to spit on the stone. When I asked him why he had done this he told me that is just what the enemy had done, but what he meant in fact was the enemy had been sucking the stone as he marched along at the very spot where he was standing, he had turned around and spat the stone out, causing a spurt backwards. Though the stone had long since dried out in the sun the enemy had left a small piece of date stuck to the stone, and this was attracting the flies to it. So I picked up the stone and had a look at it through the micro-glass which I always carried and sure enough there was the small piece of date attached, and to this day I will never know how he could possibly have known that this little stone amongst thousands of others was in fact a clue, but he did. In fact it was the ground spurt that he saw.

On another occasion we were doing some night tracking. How you might ask did he manage to see in the dark? Well the answer was that he felt the ground with his fingers, placing them into the marks made by the soldiers ahead of us.

## Visual Tracking Signs

We were bang on the enemy's trail when the light did come.

Many times I tried to copy him, only to end in near hysterics, most of which were performed by him. However after a time I found that I too could move along a track with a fair amount of accuracy.

One thing he did teach me which I find invaluable and that was never attempt to track directly into the sun for if you do you will surely come unstuck. If you find yourself tracking with the sun directly ahead of you then you must tread with caution for the sun tends to throw shadows all over your tracks and more often than not, can give you completely the wrong picture, and because of the shadows sharp edges become soft and soft edges tend to become longer, and as I have already explained everyone's footprint tells a story.

If you will have a look at the diagrams you will see that this is so. And should you feel the need to go out and practise then the best thing to do is to find a level piece of ground with some soft sand, remove your shoes and walk across the patch bare-footed. Place a small square of sticks around it to fence it off then peer at it through your glass. Note the smaller points such as the area covered by the toes, the imprint of the heel, how much of the foot's actual surface is actually in contact with the ground. The distance between the prints, measure. Draw a line through the centre of the prints as shown in the diagrams. Once you have done this now get a friend to do the same as you have done and look for the tell-tale signs, You will be amazed at the difference in the prints. If it is possible and you have a note-book with you then note down the other factors I mentioned such as earth spurts back or forward, outside or inside edges, front or rear depressions, short or narrow, and note the position of the sun. Having done all this next get yourself an old bicycle pump and some water. Spray the area that you have just marked and note the difference in foot patterns again. This is to simulate a person walking and his tracks being disturbed by the fall of rain, and believe it or not you can actually tell what kind of rain fell. By that I mean heavy or drizzle.

As the diagrams show there are four ways in which the foot can arch. When the foot is injured, then the whole foot posture can change. A good tracker will be able to tell you what injury to the foot the would-be suspect has.

Everyone knows that as soon as you twist or sprain your foot, you immediately take on some form of limp, and remembering what I said earlier about posture, as soon as you limp, you automatically start to help your tracker. The whole pyramid changes. Not all people with flat feet walk as if in pain. For instance ballet dancers are renowned for having flat feet, but because they are continually practicing and pushing and levering during a ballet session they have exceptionally strong muscles in their feet. Also very supple joints.

Next time you are watching a ballet dancer note the movements of the feet and see how they are able to stay in good posture and balance line. If the untrained person tried to do as they do, then very quickly he would be a mass of aches and pains.

Everyone's foot is very much like a thumb print. They are different in many ways. Long toes, fallen arches, short toes, toes in line, toes bent. Strong arches, missing toes, inside edge injuries, outside edge injuries, big feet, little feet, and many more individual marks.

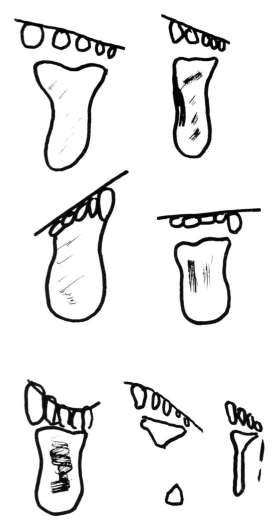

A nice steady gait, good foot pyramid, rhythmic and regular.

This tells the tracker he is fresh, unperturbed, casual. Probably not carrying any equipment. No injury, no fear, no cunning.

Note how the outer edge of the footprint is pronounced more than the inner. that there are no ground spurts to the rear or front of footprint.

From these prints with practice it is possible to get a good rough guide to the person's age, sex and height as you will learn by reading on. For the purpose of this book I shall be talking in the masculine gender (in particular reference tracking).

43

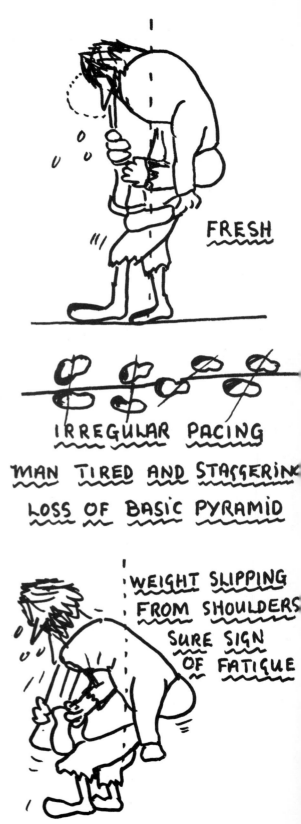

FRESH

IRREGULAR PACING

MAN TIRED AND STAGGERING

LOSS OF BASIC PYRAMID

WEIGHT SLIPPING
FROM SHOULDERS
SURE SIGN
OF FATIGUE

## Visual Tracking Signs

Here the picture shows the man carrying a weight on his back.

Once again the posture line changes. This time forwards. If the weight is directly over the man's shoulders then he is able to lift great weights this way. If the man is fit then he is able to go great distances without putting the weight down. However, if unfit then he quickly starts to waver and become very erratic on his feet, and this shows in his footprints. In this instance he will start to turn his feet inwards and the weight will have transferred to his toes. Women do not have the staying power of men so if you were tracking a woman then you would find lots of put down marks.

Because the man's weight is now over his toes the ground spurts will now be going backwards and as before the stride paces will have shortened with the weight on his back and as the man gets tired his head starts to go down so once again the line becomes erratic. All these things are tell tale signs to the tracker, and don't forget what I said earlier, every move he makes from the natural upright position he starts to help the tracker.

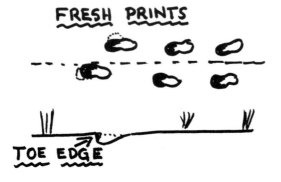

FRESH PRINTS

TOE EDGE

44

## Visual Tracking Signs.

Here the man's centre of balance is shown going backwards. This will make him dig in his heels and turn out his feet as shown. In this position it is very difficult to lift the legs high, so what happens is the man tends to turn out his feet and drag the heels to compensate for the loss of his balance. Another thing is that it is very difficult to walk in a straight line for any distance. The greater the weight the more the man's feet begin to splay out. Another give-away here is that the heels spurt forwards not leaving a clean cut edge as they would if the man's posture was normally upright.

An interesting thing here also is it is practically impossible for a woman to carry a heavy weight of any description in this way.

Later on in the book I will be comparing differences between a woman's and a man's tracks, and believe me you will be surprised at just how much difference there is.

The more the weight the smaller the man's stride. The best place to practise this yourself is either on a soft sand bed, or in the snow.

IRREGULAR PACING
LOSS OF THE BASIC
PYRAMID

WOMEN FIND
CARRYING IN
THIS POSITION
VERY DIFFICULT
FOR VERY
FEW ARE
STRONG ENOUGH
IN THE ARMS
AND SHOULDERS

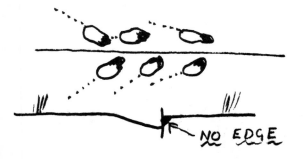

NO EDGE

# Visual Tracking Signs

A sure way of telling whether or not a sign/track is and old one is if embedded in the surface there are bits of grass or fine foliage.

If they are found to be fresh and simply lying on the surface, then providing no heavy rain has fallen they will quickly dry up and blow away. But the fact that they are embedded shows they have been there for a while. Possibly two or three days or more.

Spatter marks over the print tell the tracker that the heavy rain that fell was only for a few moments. The centre and the edge of the print will have what looks like small volcanoes.

In this case the print is completely covered with water and the edges have lost their sharpness. This tells the tracker that heavy rain fell, and it now makes it difficult to to tell just how old the tracks are. If the water is cloudy then the print could be only a few minutes old. If clear, then it could have been standing for a day or more.

Should the water show any signs of colouring on the surface this is also a sign that the person leaving it possibly wore some kind of foot covering. More probably a shoe, and this shoe or boot had some kind of protection on it, possibly boot polish.

If the front edge of the print is found to have been flattened out, and the rear end smoothly rounded, then this tells the tracker that after the person made the track there was a movement on the track surface by the wind, and if the surface is dry then the tracker can tell whether the wind was accompanied by rain.

**All this of course takes practise and lots of patience**

# SIMPLE TRACKING HINTS

**1/.** <u>LOOK FOR FRESH SIGNS</u>

TRACKS    DROPPINGS    FLIES

**2/.** <u>STALK DONT WALK</u>

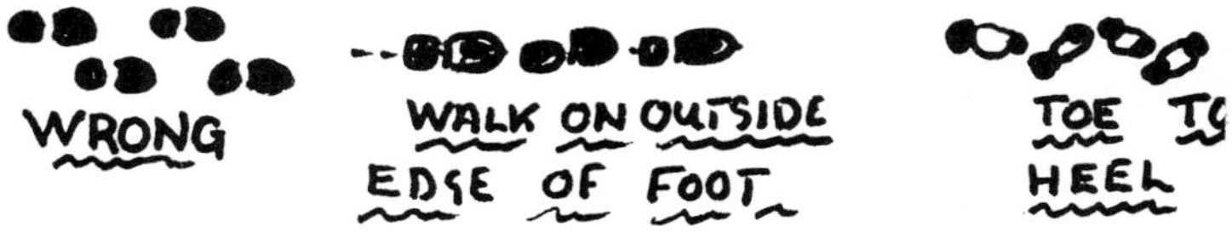

<u>WRONG</u>    <u>WALK ON OUTSIDE EDGE OF FOOT</u>    <u>TOE TO HEEL</u>

**3/.**

A.    <u>MAKE AS LITTLE NOISE AND MOVEMENT AS POSSIBLE</u>

B.    <u>IF POSSIBLE TRACK ALONE</u>

**4/.**

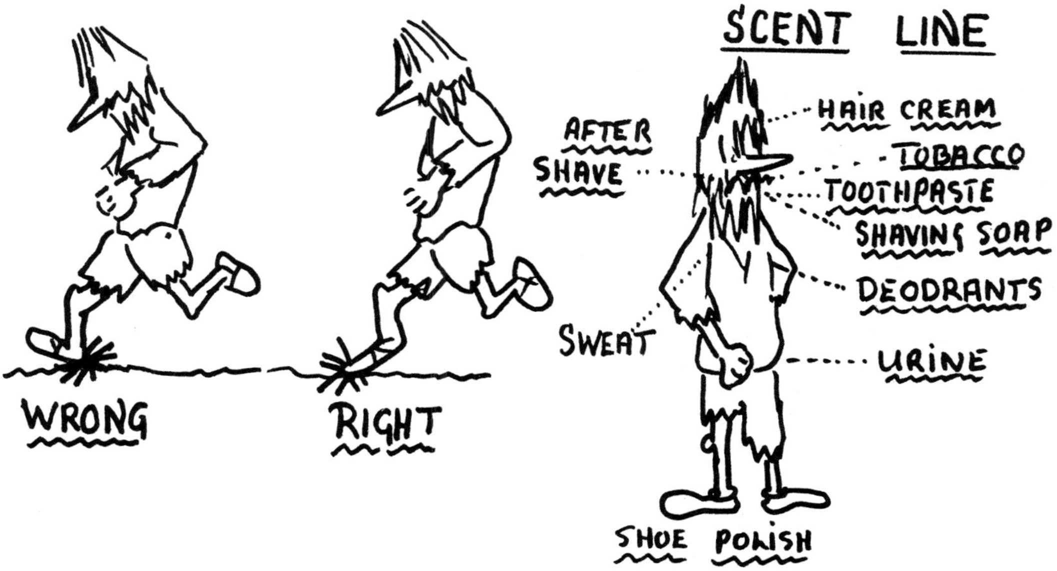

<u>SCENT LINE</u>

HAIR CREAM
TOBACCO
AFTER SHAVE
TOOTHPASTE
SHAVING SOAP
DEODRANTS
SWEAT
URINE

<u>WRONG</u>    <u>RIGHT</u>

SHOE POLISH

## <u>REMEMBER</u>

<u>KNOW YOUR STUFF AND NEVER BLUFF</u>

# Simple Tracking Hints

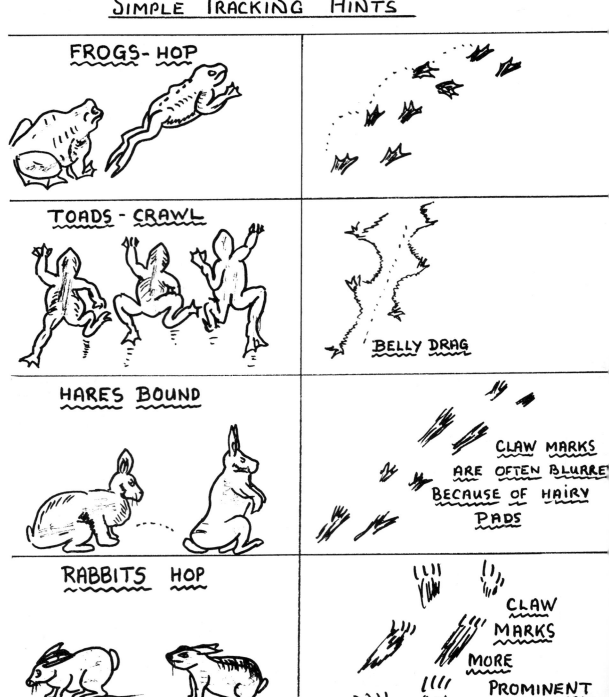

FROGS- HOP

TOADS - CRAWL

BELLY DRAG

HARES BOUND

CLAW MARKS
ARE OFTEN BLURRE
BECAUSE OF HAIRY
PADS

RABBITS HOP

CLAW
MARKS
MORE
PROMINENT

## Visual Tracking

If you can avoid it never track directly looking into the sun. The best time for you to follow a particularly difficult trail is at mid-day though of course this is not always possible I know.

Tracking into the sun presents many problems with the shadows and the signs. The sharpness tends to become a blurr and of course looking directly into the sun puts a tremendous strain on your eyes. It also seems to make things look further away than they actually are.

I have known visual trackers working in the jungle cover no more than a couple of hundred yards and have to sit down completely exhausted.

The strain of physically looking down all the time and trying to work out the signs coupled with the fact that they were actually following a live enemy were very demanding indeed, and not for one minute could they relax or rest. However, all tracking need not be so arduous.

See diagram.

If you can see the signs well ahead and you know that they are genuine then move forwards on to them. There is no need to keep looking down directly at your feet all the time. This can be very tiring and slow the tracker down considerably.

If the sun is too strong then wait a while. Better to be safe than sorry.

## Trail Markers Used by Trackers.

Here I have noted down a few of the common markers used by trackers the world over.

Some of these are practiced by the scout movements all the time, and more often than not, they use them to teach and occupy young scouts when on their annual meetings. I have seen the

same markers used in America, New Zealand, Australia, Germany, and even in Hong Kong, with devastating effect

Here are the ones used mostly by the scout federation.

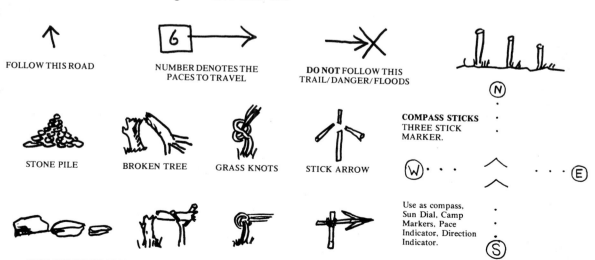

FOLLOW THIS ROAD

NUMBER DENOTES THE PACES TO TRAVEL

DO NOT FOLLOW THIS TRAIL/DANGER/FLOODS

COMPASS STICKS THREE STICK MARKER.

STONE PILE    BROKEN TREE    GRASS KNOTS    STICK ARROW

Use as compass, Sun Dial, Camp Markers, Pace Indicator, Direction Indicator.

THIS DIRECTION FORWARD.    FOLLOW TO THE RIGHT/LEFT.

AS SOON AS YOU CHANGE YOUR POSTURE. YOU CHANGE YOUR PRINTS

## Tracking

As I have said earlier the moment that the person tries to outwit you by changing his own tracks, then he is in fact helping you, as the sketch drawing will explain—

## Posture.

Man's posture can change suddenly through many reasons.

Sickness, injury, cunning (walking/running/hard or slow).

Carrying too much weight either forward or backward, use of aids and of course the weather.

Once again it is almost impossible for man to travel across any ground without leaving some form of track. Unless:

a. He is using some kind of aid to transport himself across.

b. He is travelling bare footed across exceptionally hard and smooth terrain. but even then if you are close behind him, the signs will be there (sweat).

Remember what I said? The thought transference can also help you. Try to remember just when you think you switched on to him, about what time, and when you come to the change in tracks (if any) see how far out you were.

Man is a creature of habit and one of our very dominant habits right from birth is good posture and balance.

Now have a good look at the diagrams and see how the posture changes, and indeed with each change how it can help the tracker.

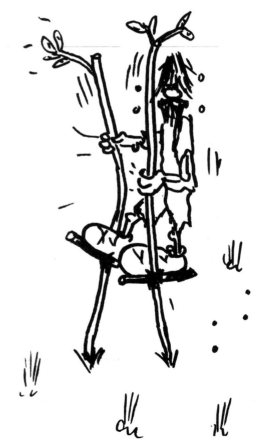

Here is a simple test that you can carry out yourself that will give you a little confidence in your tracking ability.

As I said earlier I had the good fortune to work with some of the worlds best trackers and it was interesting to learn all the many different skills that each one uses.

Find yourself an area of soft sand about twelve foot long and about six feet wide. Walk as normal down one side and have your eyes closed. Turn around and alongside the tracks you have just made do the same thing, only this time keep the eyes open. You will be amazed at the difference in your prints. You will find that one of your feet shows a definite turn outwards, this is a weakness in the foot muscles and when the foot gets tired, it will in fact turn out more than normal, and it is this defect that makes a person wander to either the right or the left. It shows even more so when the person becomes fully tired and has to lift his foot and leg to walk (walking on heather and moorland for instance puts lots of strain on the lower limbs and especially when walking in the dark or fog then one can see just how you are pulled). Look at your own prints and relate your own defect. When I teach my students I call it a (bent) you can soon check your bent by simply taking off one of your old shoes and looking at the pattern where the shoe has worn down.

Another peculiarity is that if you try to walk blindfolded for a short distance say about thirty metres you either do one of two things. You either go off in the first ten fifteen feet on to your bent, or you will almost certainly go off around the twenty five to thirty mark. With the first one, you tend to go off slightly stepping sideways as you go, or in the second one you seem to go off almost at right angles.

## Finding Direction.

Rather than go into great detail about the earth's rotation and axis I feel that this chapter would be best suited to diagrams alone. Not only are they easier to follow, but they can be used for quick reference by the survivor.

We know that the sun rises in the east and sinks in the west. We also know that the earth's rotation is on an imaginary axis which turns the earth's surface into and away from the sun at regular intervals. We call these intervals "days". As the earth rotates so at different times it tilts towards the sun and at other times away from the sun, and so by doing this we are able to get our different climatic seasons.

As I have already explained, for the purpose of this book alone, this is sufficient information on the earth's rotation.

As the seasons change so does the foliage. All of these things are equally important to the survivor. Another interesting thing about the position of the earth to the sun is no matter where we are in the world, except true north and south when the sun rises it will always rise in the east, and if we are north of the equator then the sun will always be south of us when it passes above us, and by the

same token it will always be north of us when we are south of the equator. (see diagram) but only at mid-day local time.

The scientists split the world into a series of imaginary lines, three in particular. We know these as the Tropic of Cancer, The Equator and the Tropic of Capricorn.

The dictionary defines these as three celestial imaginary lines around the earth's surface running parallel to each other and from east to west. The northern one is called the Tropic of Cancer.

As we move around from the sun's rays turning a complete circle we come to the darker side, away from the sun. This gives us our night. The whole circle complete gives us 360° a full circle. To turn the full 360° takes 24 hours.

Why is it then that if it takes 24 hours to do a full turn do we get a winter and summer sun? Why is every day not the same, well the answer lies in the earth's rotation.

As the earth rotates around the sun on its axis it in fact tilts towards the sun more during the summer months than it did in the winter and the further away from the sun's glare we go, the longer the nights. This again is best explained by the diagrams.

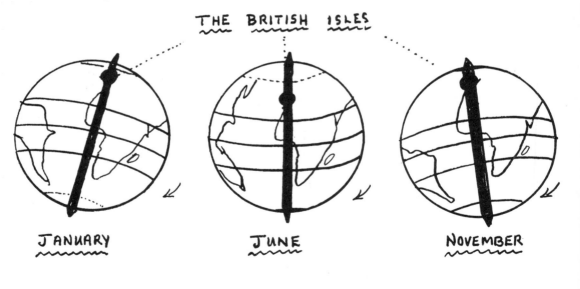

THE BRITISH ISLES

JANUARY          JUNE          NOVEMBER

THE FURTHER AWAY WE TURN FROM THE SUN'S RAYS
THE COLDER IT GETS

# SEMAPHORE  HAND  SIGNALS

READY   A   B   C   D   E   F

G   H   I   J   K   L   M

N   O   P   Q   R   S   T

U   V   W   X   Y   Z

## MORSE  CODE

| | | | |
|---|---|---|---|
| A •— | B —••• | C —•—• | D —•• |
| E • | F ••—• | G ——• | H •••• |
| I •• | J •——— | K —•— | L •—•• |
| M —— | N —• | O ——— | P •——• |
| Q ——•— | R •—• | S ••• | T — |
| U ••— | V •••— | W •—— | X —••— |
| Y —•—— | Z ——•• | | |

# KNOW YOUR SIGNALS

**Shape** — FLAGS, CLOTHING

FOOT PRINTS STONES ETC. — STONES

**Shine** — GLASS, TORCH

TIN — WATCH — GLASSES

**Shadow** — SOS

**Silhouette** — CHOP MARKS, MARKER STICKS, KITE, STREAMERS, FIRE

**Space** — RIVER STREAMERS

**Movement** — WEIGHT, FLAG, RAFT

**Noise** — FLARE/EXPLOSIVE, WHISTLE, BANGING, TIN

54

FLOATING FIRE RAFT

STONE    FIRE    LOG PLATFORM

BURN..... ANIMAL FAT.
RUBBER    GREEN FOLIAGE.

## Signalling by Improvisation

It is very strange how one adapts to the use of survival aids when one is in another country. For instance in the jungle most noises travel hardly any distance at all while banging on a hollowed-out log seems to carry a long way very effectively. In the desert, just the opposite occurs. Sound seems to work best if you can relate some form of movement to it, whilst movement on its own seems to bring its own noise, also on the sea people who have been adrift for long periods of time tell me that though they could hear things long before they could in fact see them they could not put shape or indeed colour to the noise until they could actually see the thing itself. So for this chapter I intend to try to explain to you some of the signalling devices that I have used myself. Some may amuse you while others I'm sure will have you thinking.

## Remember the Golden Rule
### SHAPE  SHINE  SHADOW  SILHOUETTE
### SPACE  MOVEMENT  NOISE

All these factors put into your survival techniques will help get fast results for you.

People who are hoping to be rescued must try to put themselves in the position of the rescue party. What would you be looking for if you were in charge of the rescue party? What, where and how?

## Signalling (Flags)

The use of flags as an aid for signalling is probably as old as man himself. Whether they be stationary on top of a post, or waved backwards or forwards by the would-be signaller. Either way they attract attention by movement and sight and that is what we need.

Once again good siting is important and of course colour where possible.

White on white snow for instance is not nearly as effective as say orange or red whilst white in the jungle stands a far better chance than dark colours. White on choppy water is also not very effective especially if the water is covered in white cap waves. So think before you start, and as with all methods of signalling have as many bits and pieces working for you as you can afford.

I know of an American serviceman who while working in Vietnam told me about an excellent method of flag signalling that he came across being used by the Vietcong.

The system though primitive was very effective. If they wanted to warn another village for instance further down the country about possible raiders or forthcoming American patrols they simply built a small platform as described in the fishing chapter (fish skiff) tie a couple of leaves and floated it down river. Two leaves on the skiff meant the Americans were coming, one leaf the Vietcong.

When you think about this, this is an excellent method of letting people know down stream that someone is there. The Chinese do the same thing with kites only they tie bows on the tails of the kites to signify different enemy. The leaves of course can be replaced by either bits of clothing or even written messages. In all nations in all countries most big cities are built and thrive along the main river system so eventually this signalling system would reach someone.

Remember what I said earlier about most rescue teams using water ways for recognition, sooner or later someone will see and someone will act.

GET WHERE
YOU CAN BE
SEEN

LISTEN
FOR REPLY

CHOOSE A SAFE
VANTAGE POINT
TO LOOK OUT
FROM

## Signalling (The Whistle)

For the survivor a very effective means of signalling, and of course can be used in most terrains.

The sound of the whistle for instance over the water surface is very loud and audible especially over enclosed waters. While in the jungle during the day when all the insects and the birds are buzzing around then the whistle amongst the trees tends to be lost.

Always keep the whistle on you. I find to suspend it from my neck by a piece of cord the best.

During my army days we used often to practice stand to and stand down while on exercise. Generally this would be first and last light or China time as it is often called in the services. This is the supposed time when the Chinese armies like to make their attacks.

First thing in the morning then is not a very good time to waste your energy. Certainly sound off a couple of times just in case anyone is around but don't waste too much energy. Prepare for the day.

Sunset is another bad time for sound. Most people mentally and physically are preparing for the night and rescue teams for instance would be standing down and re-organising for the next day's search. However, once again nothing ventured nothing gained.

Remember the international code: six short blasts, about three seconds between each blast. Wait a few minutes and then repeat. This will give time for your would-be rescuers to locate your noise and probably return same. Generally this is three successive blasts. Once you find that you have been heard, continue as before so that they may march in on you.

## Signalling (Stones and Sticks)

Easy to lay out and providing the area is cleared and sufficient materials are on hand an excellent form of signalling.

Remember the table for any type of signalling (Shape. Shine. Shadow. Silhouette. Space. Movement. Noise. Smell) no matter what or where you are, signalling from it fits into one of the headings above.

A simple thing like urine on snow, walking on snow or breaking of branches. Tying grass in knots, sticks standing erect on the horizon, these and many many more have all been used in the past as some form of signalling. Even parts of your under clothing used as flags. (Nothing ventured nothing gained).

Remember movement, noise and smell are the key factors for signalling. It would be very difficult indeed in the jungle to work shape, or silhouettes, especially for an aircraft looking down.

Always put yourself in the position of the people that are attempting to rescue you.

HIGH VANTAGE POINT

HOLLOW LOG

IF YOU HAVE NOTHING TO CHIP THE LOG WITH, THEN DO AS THE NATIVE DO — BURN IT OUT

## Signalling (Smoke)

Should the need for smoke signalling occur in the desert then once again use dark smoke where possible:— old tyres, car hoses, rubber material from seats, oils, greases etc. etc.

Light, wispy smoke from dry bush will not show very well when viewed from above during the day and in the evening or early morning when there is a light ground frost or mist around it is even more difficult to see.

Where possible try to get your signal fire on to high ground especially if you are expecting your rescuers to come by foot and during the evening if you have available some light clothing (parachute materials) then surround your fire with this. The fire shining through the material will give off an excellent glow very much like a beacon.

Don't be over-anxious to show your fire especially if materials are scarce. Too many would-be travellers have lit fires early in an attempt to attract attention only to find that when a possible aircraft rescue is under way that they did not have sufficient fuel to keep the signal going. However, one must remember, nothing ventured nothing gained.

Prepare the fire well before, keep the fire dry and site as high as possible. Make sure you have sufficient fuel to keep the signalling going.

## Signalling (Logs for Drums)

I would like to make this point early in this chapter so that a would-be survivor is not working under a misapprehension. Of all the many years that I have worked in the jungle at no time have I ever come across any hollowed out logs to be used as a drum as depicted by the film media.

All the jungle drums I have come across were made with loving care and workmanship.

In the jungle the sound of the drum carries much further than a gun, blast, or whistle. So for the natives who have no means of electricity this form of communication has to be effective and efficient.

The simplest method of making a drum from a log is to chip and burn. This takes a little time but if the situation demands it, it is well worth the effort.

The biggest task is finding a suitable log not too small or too large. It is important that the log has no signs of rottenness and withering. Around the waters-edge is probably your best bet for finding a ready-made suitable log; one that has probably been washed downstream during a torrential storm; also working by the river edge it is far easier to move the log to where you need to work on it.

While the log is being hollowed out by the fire of course it is still working as your signalling guide. Hot embers at night burning inside the log as well as glowing also work as a means of recognition.

## Compass Sticks

As you can see by the simple drawings the use of the compass sticks are very simple indeed and also very effective.

If you take the time to site your sticks correctly then they can provide you with other information other than telling the time. For instance by placing the largest of the three sticks away from your base and in line with the others. Then when returning to your base it is far easier to see the bigger stick than the smaller one. When you do arrive at your sticks, if you have lined them up correctly then you should be able to look along them and find the exact location of your shelter.

Place them as near as possible in the positions of the compass. By this I mean North, South, East and West, also place them all the same distance away from the camp by stride measure.

CAMP AREA

# TRACKING IN THESE CONDITIONS

HEAVY RAIN

FOGGY CONDITIONS

## REMINDERS

In any area where man or game is present there can be many different kinds of signs, or clues which will aid the tracker. An untrained tracker may only see two or three of these signs and even a trained tracker may on first sight see only five or six.

The following simple rules will assist you and make tracking much easier.

*THE GOLDEN RULE — PATIENCE*
**STOP — LOOK — LISTEN.**

*Think Tracking* — use your own natural insticts.
*Think animal* — (Know your stuff. Do not Bluff).

The weather obviously plays a very important part in tracking and the following notes may help.

**FOGGY CONDITION**
Birds tend not to fly and game is especially cautious and noises seem to be exaggerated.

**HEAVY RAIN**
Fresh tracks have been washed away, bent and moved foliage quickly returns to its original shape and is not easily broken (this can make sounds either for or against the tracker). Most game goes to ground and previous urine and excrement traces lose their smell.

**AFTER RAIN**
All man and game movement will leave tracks, lots of noise for or against the tracker and game is abundant immediately after a storm.

## Survival Navigation

Probably the world's first most accurate compass or means of finding true direction was the use of the fire lines. The Aborigines were the fore-runners of this and even today they still use it.

Basically all it entails is the burning of fires in a straight line at given distances. This method works during the day or night. It is not unlike the method of the Arabs when they use sticks or flags.

Remember Scott of the Antartic? He used the flag system.

To keep the fires burning the Aborigines burn a plant called Spinifex — this plant has great burning properties and gives off large amounts of smoke. Of course under survival conditions anything that burns well and gives off sufficient smoke will do just as well.

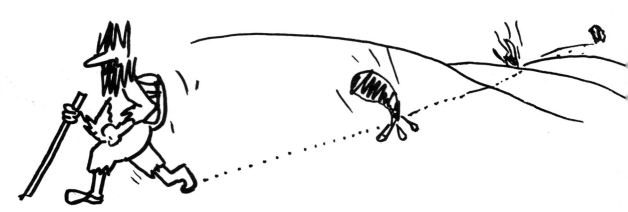

Another excellent method of survival navigation is the three man and a rope system. This also can be used either in the day or night.

Simply all it entails is that the three men hold the rope in their hands, left or right but they must all have it in the same one. One standing behind the other. They can either move off all together or one at a time to a given distance. Any directional change at all will register in the hand held section of the rope with the others. The same system may also be used without the rope. But at night very strict control must be maintained.

## The Mirror

Probably one of the most effective and widely used methods of signalling in the world of survival.

Reflective signalling has been recorded as far back as the ancient Briton's time. The reflection of a fire glow on the evening sky line, the glint of a warrior's sword, and the shimmering glint of water have been with us for many thousands of years now, and have changed very little.

A slight modern improvement on the sword reflector is the ever popular mirror. This pointed at the rescuers and catching the sun's glare can be seen for over thirty miles. The mirror reflection techniques were introduced into the world's fighting forces many long years ago not only as a means of communication but also as a warning system.

Probably the world's first known signallers to actually send off messages by this method in the form of actual communication were the Roman armies. Historians tell us that certain members of this army were in fact taught to send and receive messages, and they were probably the fore-runners of what we now know as Morse Code.

Later on we were to see the mirror used by the ever popular Indians seen on our T.V. screens.

The modern armed services still rely a great deal on this method of signalling and in all armed services throughout the world fighting men are still taught morse code signalling by the use of reflection be it the sun's rays, the artificial light of batteries or electricity. All I feel will be with us for a long while to come yet. In the case of the sun it's free and easy to use. In the modern world both batteries and electricity are reasonably easy to come by.

However, we are under survival conditions and we do not have on tap batteries or electricity so we have to start improvising. As I said earlier reflections can be seen for many miles providing the sun is shining strongly enough and even on a dull overcast day you can still get a small amount of reflection from your mirror if set correctly.

## Direction Finding

Finding the north or the south by the use of your watch and the sun is a simple but very effective method taught all over the world, not only to the military but to all outdoor instructors, including scout, cub and the many youth leaders who in their turn do an excellent job of work in their outdoor training.

Finding True North, Greenwich Mean Time.

Point the hour hand of the watch at the sun, laying the watch as flat as you can, by simply tilting your wrist. Then halve the distance between the hour hand and twelve, as shown. This will give you a North-South line.

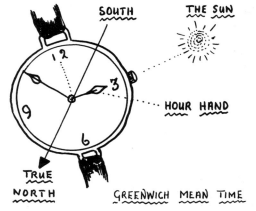

Finding South, British Summer Time.

Follow the same procedure as for G.M.T. but this time halve the distance between one o'clock and the hour hand. See diagram.

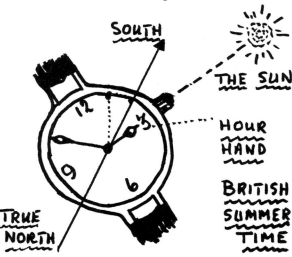

## Survival Navigation

To find the north in the southern region you need to locate the Southern Cross. There are other groups of stars that one can refer to but the cross is probably the simplest one to find and work from.

Beware here for one can get the false cross confused with the southern one. A few simple tricks will help you to locate the right one and they are:— The false cross is much more closely packed than the southern one, also the false cross will show just below and to the right of the southern one. The southern one also has a couple of pointers to help you locate it and these locater stars are also included in the location position of the south.

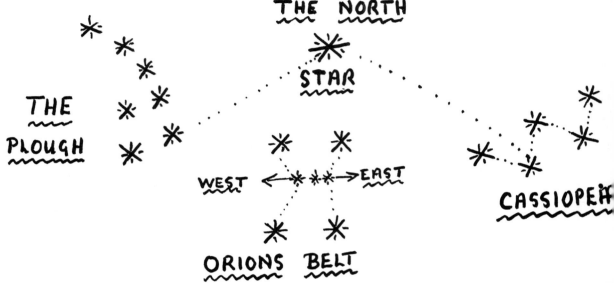

THE NORTH STAR

THE PLOUGH

WEST ← ✳✳✳ → EAST

ORIONS BELT

CASSIOPEA

In the northern hemisphere the north star can be located from the Plough, (Dipper), Orion's Belt, and Cassiopea. These are three groups of stars and all have pointers that point to the North Star.

It is worth noting that Orion's Belt rises in the east and sinks in the west and at all times the actual belt always runs true east, west. See Diagrams.

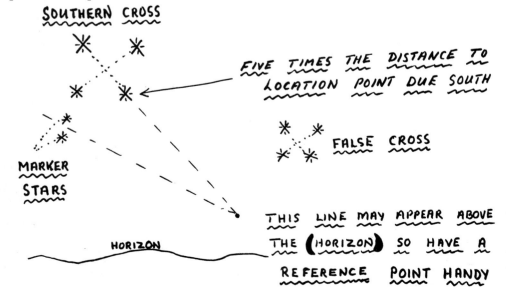

SOUTHERN CROSS

FIVE TIMES THE DISTANCE TO LOCATION POINT DUE SOUTH

FALSE CROSS

MARKER STARS

THIS LINE MAY APPEAR ABOVE THE (HORIZON) SO HAVE A REFERENCE POINT HANDY

HORIZON

1. FINDING EAST. WEST. LINE
2. FINDING NORTH. SOUTH LINE } SOUTHERN HEMISPHERE
3. FINDING THE TIME

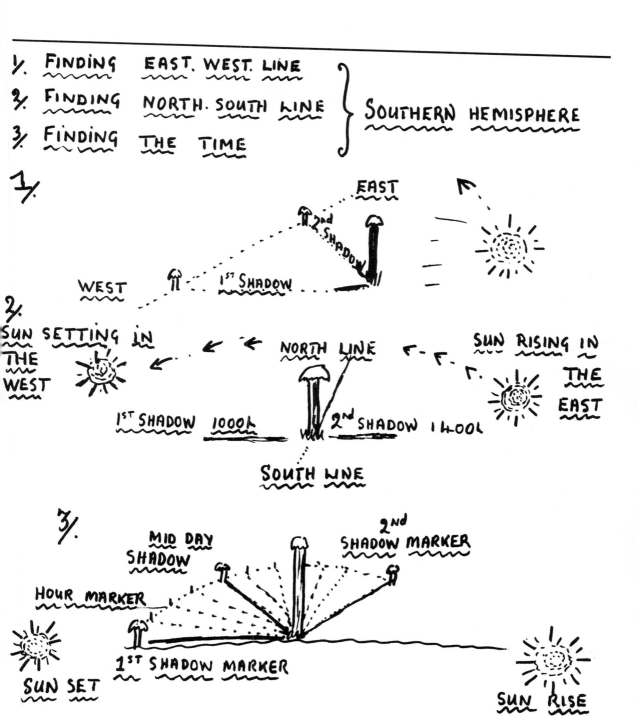

## Survival Navigation

The use of the Shadow Stick is well known but is often confused. By this means one method is used for finding east west line. Another for giving you a rough time guide and another for telling north and south.

In all cases it is best done on a level piece of ground cleared of scrub. You will also need a straight stick about three feet long though this is not essential.

## Survival Navigation

As well as the use of the sun and stars for navigation finding, the moon and indeed many plants and herbs can also aid the survivor. And if one has followed the migration of certain birds and animals one can also get a rough guide. The list is endless, and as with all survival skills I strongly recommend that you spend a few worthwhile days and nights out practising.

Study the moon. Watch from where it comes and where it goes. Note the time of day you can see it. Make a note of the months and seasons that you see it. Just where is it when it is a full moon and where it is when only a quarter one. How many times a year can one see a full moon for instance. Only by reading up on it and actually going out and studying it will you gain any confidence in it as a survival navigator.

Every schoolboy knows that the moon changes from a full one to nothing at all. Why is this? Well, when the moon is on the same side of the earth as the sun, the shaded side is towards the earth. When on the opposite side of the earth to the sun then one sees a full moon surface. This of course is caused by the sun's reflection.

If the moon rises in time with the sun then it will show a full moon.

If the moon rises after the sun it will show illuminated on your east side.

If the moon rises before the sun, it will show illuminated on your west side.

See simple diagram.

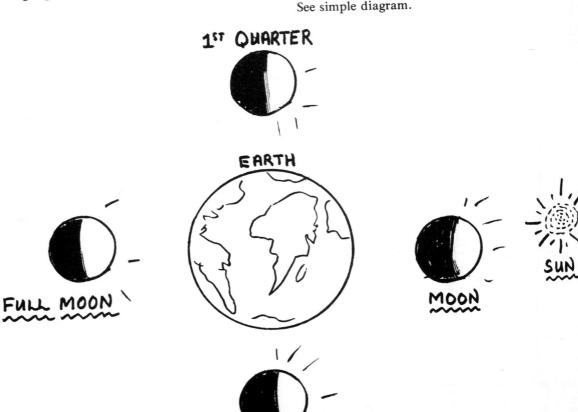

## Explosives for Signalling

Flares of any description are an excellent means of signalling. If the flare is the hand-held version then ensure that it can be seen clearly, for in the jungle, even at night, it is difficult for an aircraft that is 'hopping' along to spot the glare when under thick foliage. Not only the glare can be seen by the rescuers but also the smoke. In some cases the smoke screen from certain flares can be quite strong.

Any form of torch is good. Whether it is the type that requires batteries, or a simple hand made one of a stick and an oily rag, or animal fat. Save it until you are sure that you can be seen once the torch is lit. From my own experience I have found that cheap battery torches nearly always seem to go wrong just when you need them the most. If you are going to carry a torch with you in your survival kit then choose a good one, and preferably one that is waterproofed, and unsinkable. Diver's torches are probably the best type. An old wrinkle for getting a little more from your torch batteries is to warm them, either in an oven or on a stone for about forty-five minutes or so. This seems to give them some extra life. Keep the batteries completely dry at all times. Some makers of certain batteries claim that this is not always necessary, but I have not yet come across a make that has not let me down when it has been subjected to damp.

When working with explosives extra caution must be used always, as with the flares. The functions of explosives are two-fold. One, a brilliant flash, which is instantaneous, and two, the actual bang or blast.

The sound of jungle drums carry great distances, but the sound of a single blast seems to disappear almost at once, but if the explosive is used near a stream or river, on the bank, then results are much better. Don't waste your explosives by throwing them into the water. If you need to get the sound out into the middle of the stream then build yourself a raft, or some means of floating the sound out into the middle.

Do not waste your valuable explosives by using them near waterfalls or rapids. The noise of the rushing water will only drown out half of the sound and the air that has been disturbed by the waterfall will be damp and will probably cut down a lot of the blast.

Petrol or oils, of course, are excellent ways of attracting attention once they have been ignited. But as I have said before, with anything as highly inflammable as petrol, then take full precautions. In the jungle the simplest way of using petrol for signalling is to light a fire and burn green wood or foliage. If you have some oil handy, say from your vehicle or plane or whatever, then a simple but very effective method is to find a spot in the river that is fairly calm, mix the petrol and the oil together, soak a couple of logs in the mixture, light and float away from the bank. You can, of course, pour some of the mixture onto the surface of the water and then light it. This will burn fine for a while, and will give far better results than lighting it under thick jungle foliage. If in the desert then almost certainly the best method is to try and contain as much of the mixture as you can in a small container, as with the desert burner and light it. It is not a good practice to light the fire then drop small amounts of sand into the container, as I have heard would-be instructors tell. This will only smother the fire and put it out. So always ensure that you mix both the sand and petrol or oil well before lighting.

Remember that most rescue teams work in given areas as per their direction teams, and they nearly always work their boundaries either in mountain ranges or from river to river, so they will be watching streams and rivers nearly all the time. Give them time, and assistance. Once you think that you have been seen then stay where you are until they arrive. All too often the would-be survivor thinks that he has not been spotted and, feeling down in the dumps, wanders off only to become lost even further. With an aircraft, once they think they have spotted you, they in turn will be notifying their base of your location so may seem to be flying on and completely ignoring you. Work as a team and things will work for you. Above all don't panic and injure yourself by dashing off into the bush or desert trying to shout the aircraft down. If he has seen you then he will come back.

## Survival Navigation

I cannot possibly give you all the many thousands of herbs and plants that guide us in our direction finding, but, in all parts of the world there are forms of plant life that do just this.

Here, in Europe, we have herbs, grasses and trees that face only one direction when in bloom. To read these plants and signs one must learn to recognise them fully, for in this country in particular we have very strong variable winds, which, over a period of time tend to bend some plants and trees in completely the wrong direction to which they want to go. As I mentioned earlier in the book all plants tend to look for the last light, and in so doing may turn away from their natural growing habitat. A classic example is the common rhubarb. In its natural state it spreads well out in all directions, whilst under forced control will grow as straight as a pole.

Certain species of the animal and bird kingdom also give the survivor a rough direction.

Swallows, for instance, will not nest facing north, and lapwings do not like to face into the prevailing winds. Observe a pheasant when roosting and you will notice it nearly always turns facing due south east. This is because it is an early riser and uses the light from the sun in wakening. Watch a hedgehog and see how it turns to the early morning sunshine and follows it around as the warmth stirs insects and creatures in its diet.

## PREVAILING WINDS

TREES

GRASSES

PLANTS

TREES

MOSS

# 3  Trapping

## Trapping for Survival

It has been difficult in compiling this book to stop myself from going too deeply into trapping. As well as my survival skills, I have, over the years, made a very deep and comprehensive study of trapping. So you must bear with me if you feel that I should have dealt with trapping in more depth in the book.

This book is purely for the survivor and is not intended to teach ruthless unnecessary killing of game and animals. In fact, I think I am probably one of the strongest supporters of conservation you will find. Many is the time when I have been on one of my expeditions that I have deliberately put myself into a survival situation and restricted myself to only living off the local vegetation.

In my survival centre I have posters from the R.S.P.C.A., explaining quite clearly the legalities involved in the practice of killing, trapping, poisoning or removing any form of wild life unless official permission has been given. Quite often I have had visits from the senior R.S.P.C.A. officers. However, the officers point out that under survival conditions the need to survive must come first. Throughout the world there is a tremendous battle going on to try to eliminate the greed of the professional poachers who do irreparable damage to the wild animal world. I do not consider myself a poacher, but more of a teacher (through practical work) of the countryside. Many professional naturalists have been on my courses and have told me afterwards how much they have enjoyed the chance to try new-found skills for themselves and new things about the countryside. To this day one friend of mine now uses one of the many traps I showed him to catch and study certain animals, and indeed has written one or two excellent books on certain species, because he has been able to catch without killing.

Once I was asked if I would like to go on a safari whilst in Africa, but I quickly declined. There is enough killing in the world without me adding to it. Even in my own village I refuse to go on fox-hunts. And when my courses are running I am the first to admit that I buy all my game for the courses from the local butcher.

## The Predatory British

Contrary to popular belief, on my travels around the world, I have never found the art of trapping more widely used than here in England. History shows that we were one of the world's most vicious and destructive nations in the use of trapping and snaring. One has only to read about our ancestors who colonised country upon country killing buffalo/seal/elephant/tiger/crocodile etc., to find that they used some of the world's most vicious and deadly methods of trapping animals and man to gain full control. Our museums are filled with old man and animal traps used many centuries ago and some historians claim that we were the founders of torture by the use of aids and traps.

It is strange, especially when we are now considered by the rest of the world as a nation of animal lovers, that we were once the founders of and indeed the exporters of, some of the deadliest trapping and torture devices ever thought of by mankind. It has not been my aim in this book though, to knock our ancestors nor to criticise them for giving this heritage, indeed some of the methods of trapping that they have passed on to us have proved to be of invaluable use to us in many aspects. Though the trapping and killing of any game is illegal in this country we still use some of the earlier skills left, to control the pests and vermin that very often try to get control in this country and it is still possible, in some parts of the country, to find traps and snares used in the control of vermin, though this is very strictly controlled by the R.S.P.C.A.

## Trap Setting Skills

It is important to remember, when setting your traps, the type of animal or bird you are hoping to catch.

Bird traps, for instance, need very light and in some cases intricate types of trigger mechanisms before they do their job correctly, while bigger traps for carnivorous types of animals, such as the wolf, may require strong, firm trigger mechanisms.

This is one side of the survival world that you just have to practice if you want to gain any sort of success in trapping. For instance, I always ensure that if I set any type of bird trap, that it will go off at the drop of a match box. I remember once being asked to design a trap for a very eminent T.V. personality who wanted to catch (for study only) a very small, light and exceedingly rare bird in the tropics.

It was so light in fact that it weighed no more than an empty match box, and indeed was a little smaller than the average match box. With this information I set about building a small, light, cage type of trap as shown in the trapping section of the book. The bird also needed plenty of water, so knowing these things I built the pyramid type trap. The trap was a success, but needed plenty of skill to set it each time.

When setting traps for bigger game the same things must be considered. For instance the wolf. It likes to tear its kill. It will not hesitate to charge in for the kill. Once it has got hold, it does not like to let go. It is very strong, very cunning and when cornered, very very dangerous. So things like this must be considered when preparing your trap. This is one of the main reasons why beginners have so very little success each time they try the trap.

As I said earlier, an important factor to consider is the setting of your traps. The first time I send off my students to practise their trapping they invariably end in failure and I consider this as a very important part of my teachings, for if the students were to achieve success each time they set a trap this would give them a false sense of security. One golden rule I always tell my students is: "Wrong siting and incorrect setting" will not give you success. Think before you set. Smell, type place and time are just as important as the making of the trap.

## Traps and Trapping

In my many years as a survival instructor, I have tried not to specialise in any one aspect of survival. However, I think it is only right to say that the art of trapping caught my imagination most. In my younger days there was nothing I enjoyed more than to go off into the woods and practise various trapping techniques. Though I was born in a town, every spare minute I could get, away from home, you would find me either out in the nearest woods, or on the moors setting traps and practising my tracking skills.

I have many books on the art of surviving and indeed some good ones on tracking, but the number of books written on trapping and actual setting of traps I could count on one hand. Why, I do not know and in all the countries I have travelled I still could not find much information, so it is with this in mind that I have decided to put down on paper for all to share, the experiences that I have gained whilst travelling the world.

Trapping, of course, is as old as man himself. As soon as man learned that meat was a source of food, then his trapping skills evolved. Not only did he trap for food but very often he would devise traps for the purpose of catching his enemy and for the protection of his food and homestead. Probably the earliest form of trapping was to try to drive either the game, or his enemy into a bog or marsh. Although this proved to be a very effective method of actually catching, it also proved to be a very dangerous way for him to get his catch out, so it is probably from this that the early stone-age 'trap pit' came. This would be a very large hole, some ten or twelve feet deep and about six feet across. Some very large and dangerous pointed stakes were in the bottom for the game to impale itself on when it fell, or was driven, into the pit.

## Try These
## Trap from a Newspaper or Bark

1.  For this you will need a sheet of paper or very thin bark, about twelve inches square.

2.  Find a spot where the birds are roosting. (The bigger the bird the easier the trap works) and bait well in advance of setting the trap.

3.  You will need something to dig a hole with. A good stout stick is ideal here, about four feet long and well sharpened at one end.

4.  Place the stick in the ground and rotate it until you have a conical shaped hole about twelve inches deep and 6 inches wide.

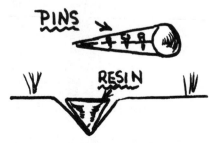

5.  Form your paper/bark into the same conical shape and pin with a small twig. Next gather some resin from any pine tree and stick this on to the inside edges of the cone.

6.  Put your bait into the bottom of the cone and leave alone. When the bird comes along he will put his head into the cone for the bait and on lifting will/or should, come out with a dunce's cap on. This will not hurt the bird and once again this is a pure survival technique that can be improvised from natural surroundings.

## The Setting and Laying of Snares

If you want to have any success at all with your trap setting it is important that you learn the correct way to make them and how to set them; for instance, the everyday common snare, which is illegal in this country and indeed in most other countries I have been in.

The making of the snare is very important. If, for instance, you want to catch a rabbit then there are a few things that you must consider, such as the weight of the animal you intend to trap, the strength of the animal, where does it live, where does it go for its food and what kind of food does it like best and last but not least, what kind of a trap or snare doe you want to use? All these things come naturally to the survivor after a couple of days alone and when you start living close to nature it is surprising how skilful you do become in a short time.

The diagrams will explain the setting of the snares for you, but you must not expect success each time. I know of a few old poachers who had great difficulty in getting any success from their snare setting in their early years, because they had not bothered to follow the few simple rules that I have mentioned, when considering setting a trap/snare. Smell is another important factor to consider, also the weather. Strong winds, for instance have many a time either set off or blown over a man's trap because of bad setting and siting. When teaching army students the basics of trapping the one thing that I insist on is : BE ANIMAL, THINK ANIMAL.

## A Water Fowl or Duck Trap

Here is another method of catching food (in this case water fowl).

My father taught me this many years ago, when I was very young. I used to practise this one for days until I had perfected it. Once again, like all traps, good siting and setting is essential. This one is so simple, yet so effective. My grandfather taught my father the uses of this trap, so I guess you could say it's been passed down from generation to generation. I have already taught my two sons.

1. First, gather three good sized sticks, about three feet long and sharpen them at both ends.

2. Now drive them into the water in the shape of a triangle leaning slightly outwards as shown in the diagram. The distance between the stakes will depend on the size of the stone, or weight you are going to use.

3. Next you need a good sized stone or weight, about 5 to 6 pounds; certainly no heavier. Its purpose is to drag the game's head down into the water and drown it. Not to sink it to the bottom.

4. At this stage you can either use a fish hook, or snare wire. If you use a fish hook, tie on the bait and the other end tie to the weight as shown in the diagram.

5. When the game takes the bait it topples the weight from the spiked sticks. This drags the game down under the water and drowns it.

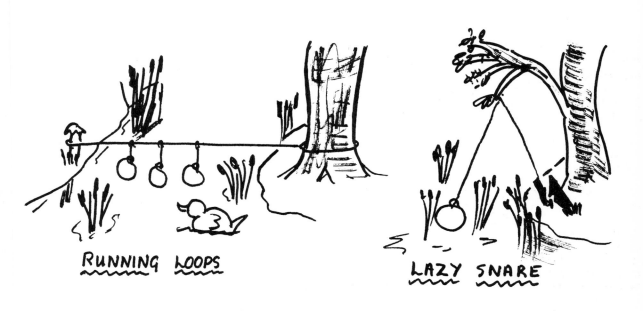

RUNNING LOOPS

LAZY SNARE

NOTHING VENTURED    NOTHING GAINED

BARBED WIRE
& FEATHERS

OLD FROG

INSECTS

GIBLETS

COTTON
WOOL

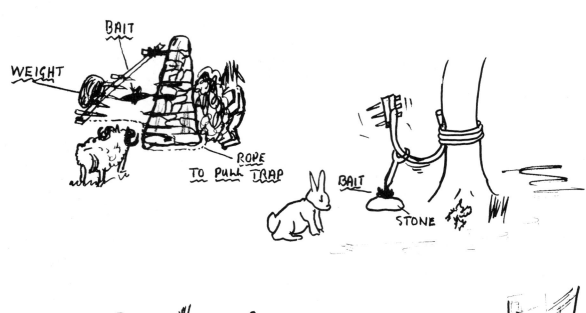

BAIT

WEIGHT

ROPE
TO PULL TRAP

BAIT

STONE

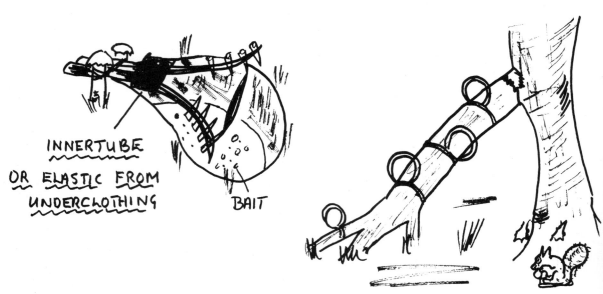

INNERTUBE
OR ELASTIC FROM
UNDERCLOTHING

BAIT

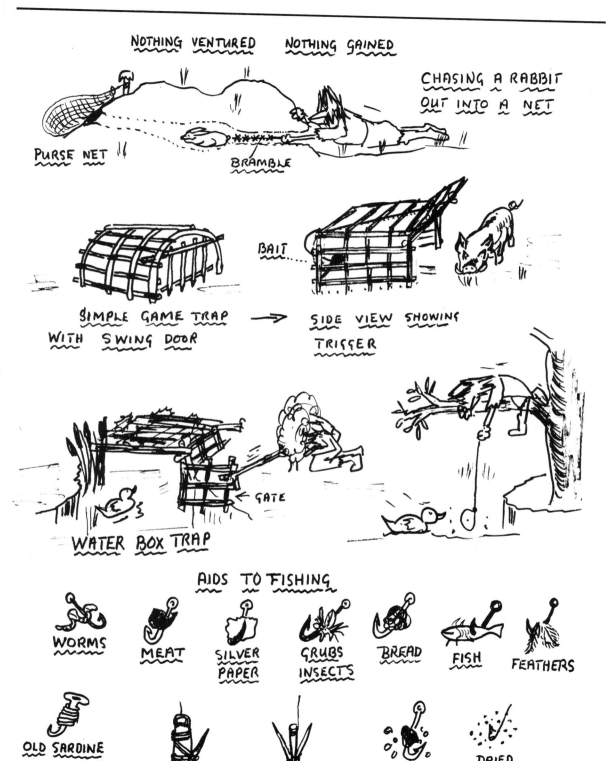

NOTHING VENTURED    NOTHING GAINED

PURSE NET

BRAMBLE

CHASING A RABBIT
OUT INTO A NET

SIMPLE GAME TRAP
WITH SWING DOOR

BAIT

SIDE VIEW SHOWING
TRIGGER

WATER BOX TRAP

GATE

AIDS TO FISHING

WORMS

MEAT

SILVER
PAPER

GRUBS
INSECTS

BREAD

FISH

FEATHERS

OLD SARDINE
CAN OPENER

PENKNIFE

FISH GAFF

HONEY

DRIED
ANIMAL DUNG

73

## Setting a Rabbit Snare on the Ground

Choose the materials that you want to make the snare with. Wire is probably the best, though good strong twine will do. Cut off a length about the length of your arm from your nose as shown.

Now cut a good strong stake to tie the snare to. Sharpen this to a point at one end.

Make sure that the snare loop is free running or you will find it snagging when pulled.

In this case we are going to put the snare on the rabbit's run, so we must consider all the things that I mentioned before.

Once you have found the run look for the 'high' and 'low' spots that the rabbit makes when he is running. (see diagram).

Drive the stake into the ground hard, trying not to disturb the trail. Set the snare as shown and remember, for success it needs to be on the 'high', four fingers high, and at this stage you can support it with a small twig if you want to. Whatever you do, do not keep going to have a look at it. Do not worry if you don't catch anything on the first day. You have probably disturbed the scent line, so you will have to wait a little longer for it to disappear.

RABBIT RUN

SIDE VIEW SHOWING HIGH AN LOW MARKS

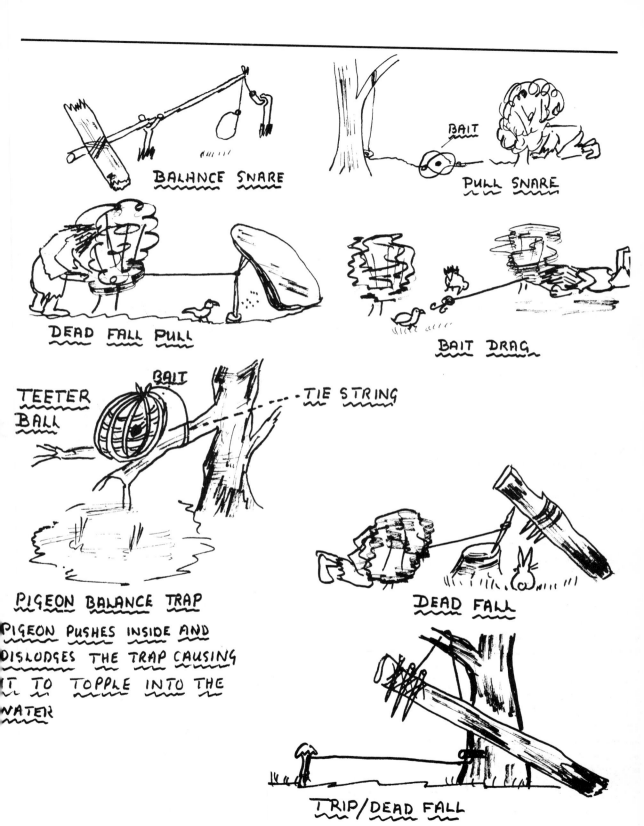

BALANCE SNARE

PULL SNARE

BAIT

DEAD FALL PULL

BAIT DRAG

TEETER BALL

BAIT

TIE STRING

PIGEON BALANCE TRAP

PIGEON PUSHES INSIDE AND
DISLODGES THE TRAP CAUSING
IT TO TOPPLE INTO THE
WATER

DEAD FALL

TRIP/DEAD FALL

DUCK FLOAT

BOTTLE HALF FILLED WITH WATER

RUBBING STICK

WEDGE

## IMPROVISED FISH SCOOPS AND GAFFS

OLD SILK STOCKING/TIGHTS PLASTIC BAG

SPEAR GAFF

BENT FORK GAFF

BARBED WIRE

MARKER AND SIGNAL FLAG

MAKE A HOLE IN THE ICE

## Skinning and Curing

The curing of skins is not so difficult under survival conditions, and after a little practice you soon find yourself becoming very expert.

There are, of course, modern clinical methods of curing, but these are very expensive and require large amounts of equipment. The survivor requires nothing more than a stone, some sand, a log and water. This, coupled with a little bit of elbow grease, will soon have your skins looking something like and ready for you to work with.

I found the easiest method was to try and remove as much of the fat and flesh from the skin as soon as possible after actually skinning the animal.

Once this has been done to your satisfaction then you can set about preparing your curing table. For this you will need some water. Preferably running water, i.e. a stream. Now find a reasonable sized stone to use as a table, or a log will do. You will also need some kind of scraper to remove the remaining fat that you may have left behind. Soak the skin thoroughly and place on your table.

Run some of the sand from the stream bed on to the skin, then start to rub and scrape. Do not press too heavily at this stage, otherwise you will find that the skin will start to roll up and may start to tear. It is also advisable at this stage, to scrape in an up and down motion rather than a circular one. Keep dipping the skin into the water to remove the waste. Remember that cold water alone will not remove the fat. This has to be done by the sand, and friction.

Once all the fat has been removed, the skin needs to be hung out to dry for a while. At this stage you will find that the skin has gone very stiff and possibly some of the animal's fur may have started to come away. Do not worry. When the skin is dried we can set about getting it nice and supple, ready for us to work with.

I have tried a couple of ways and both of them have been very effective.

Make what I can only describe as a beating table. For this I used three logs about two feet long and about six inches thick. Tie two of them together as shown. Now place the skin loosely over the logs. With your third log placed on top of the others, hold the skin in one hand, then gently draw the skin through the logs, each time turning the skin over. Once you have taken the initial stiffness out you will have to start to add more weight to the top log as you draw the skin through. This method only takes out initial stiffness, so now you will have to remove the skin from the logs and set about making it supple, over your knee. This takes a little time but after a while you will start to see the results of your efforts. You can, if the skin is still a little on the stiff side, pour some hot water over it to take out the stiffness, but do not over-do this or you will make the skin too soft and pulpy. One old Arab told me that the best water for this was in fact the natural water from your body. In other words your urine. This has natural salts in it and it helps in the processing once the skin has been softened by the water. Now place the skin back into the roller press and repeat the first part again. This method, I found, worked best on small skins like rabbit or monkey. For the larger ones like wild deer, pig, goat or sheep, I found that the hanging method worked best.

Just as I did with the first method, I ensured that the skin had been cleaned as much as possible of all surface fat. Now soak it in water for a couple of hours, remove it, place it on a hanging rack this time, as shown in the diagram.

Once this has been done and before the skin has had chance to dry off, use one of your logs to act as a beater. Do not thrash the skin too hard, otherwise you find it soon begins to stretch. Keep on beating until you have reached a reasonable standard of suppleness, then return the skin to the water to soak again. Wait another hour, then **repeat. Do** this three times.

# CURING A SKIN

BEATING TABLE.

PLACE IN A SHALLOW POOL OR STREAM

PULL

PULL THE SKIN THROUGH FOR A FEW MINUTES TO REMOVE THE INITIAL STIFNESS. THIS IS DONE BEST AFTER THE SKIN AS HAD A GOOD SOAKING FOR A COUPLE OF HOURS

ONCE THE SKIN HAS BEEN SOFTENED BY PULLING THROUGH, NOW WHILE STILL WET BEAT TO MAKE PLIABLE

## 2ND METHOD

SOAK THE SKIN WELL AFTER REMOVING ALL SURPLUS MEAT & FAT. THIS IS BEST DONE WITH SAND AND A STONE COUPLED WITH PLENTY OF ELBOW GREASE

REMOVE ALL FAT & MEAT

A BEATING FRAME

LET THE NATURAL
BODY HEAT DISPERSE
FIRST BEFORE
ATTEMPTING TO EAT
THE MEAT RAW,
A COUPLE OF
HOURS WILL DO FINE.
BUT REMEMBER
WHERE POSSIBLE
COOK FIRST.

Earlier in the book I mentioned that it is not important that you hang your meat supply out for a few days prior to eating it and this is true, for anyone who is under survival conditions just will not be able to resist the temptation of the meat hanging there anyway. However, I must say this; it is advisable for you to at least try to let the animal's natural body heat disappear before you attempt to eat it. If you do not and you start tearing away at the warm flesh, then you will probably find yourself being very ill.

At this moment in the book I think it would be appreciated if I listed all the parts of the animal that one can eat and how to cook.

I shall use the deer or venison as an example.

**Brains.** These can be washed and either fried or slowly boiled. To make the brains a little tastier, add an egg or two and some of the herbs. Scramble the lot and you have a first class meal.

**Tongue.** Wash well and then leave to soak for an hour or two. Wash again, place in cold water and bring to a boil and simmer for two to three hours. This will make it nice and tender. Again add the herbs of your choosing for taste.

**The Heart.** Remove all fibrous tissues. Cut up into small pieces and use in your stews. It can, of course, be cut up into slices and fried.

**The Liver.** Remove the gall-bladder carefully, if the animal has one, not all do. Wash well, as always. You can cook it direct on the fire, the green stick method. Cut it up into small chunks and use in your stews. Slice it and fry on any hot stone or pan. Boil it and remember to keep the butter-like substance that will come out on the top. This is of no use to you so discard it.

**The Kidneys.** Soak well in cold water, cut into small squares and place in your stew.

**The Spleen.** Wash well; boil for an hour; re-wash. Then boil again until required tenderness is reached.

**Marrow Bone.** Cover the ends of the bone with cloth; boil upright for at least two hours; remove cloth. Crack open the bone and remove the marrow. Eaten on toast this an excellent dish.

Should you have been fortunate enough to have killed any larger game, then your meat problems will be over for a while, at least for a few days anyway. However, the correct way of cutting up your meat supply is just as important as with the smaller game.

For general information I have listed what is probably the simplest and easiest method known. This will help you to identify your meat, especially when you come to curing or cooking, also for general storage, i.e. steaks, hams, surloin, etc.

Like all fresh cut meat, it is important that you have some means of storage available and possibly a curing table. If not, once the meat has gone off, if not treated, it will soon go bad, and this in turn will quickly bring unwanted visitors into your camp, ants, flies, etc.

As with any game, of course, it is important that you first gut and clean your food before you make any attempt to store or cure it.

Listed below are the meat sections you are about to cut.

## Skinning your Rabbit/Hare Correctly

If you are fortunate enough to be able to catch a rabbit/hare during your survival, then it's as well to try to kill a few myths about their edibility. The rabbit and the hare provide an excellent meal and if you are starving, it matters not one bit whether you hang your meal for a few days or eat it there and then. It will probably taste better to you anyway. In all my years of survival training I don't think I have ever hung a rabbit/hare yet.

Many experts claim that hanging the game first for a few days or so helps to give the meal a better taste. This may be so, but when you are hungry you just do not have the time. Anyway, as I have said earlier in the book, it is far better to skin your meal as soon as possible after catching it. It would be a very strong-willed person who could sit there starving knowing that only a few feet away hangs a delicious meal, skinned, just waiting to be eaten.

However, to be fair, it would be wrong of me not to mention at this stage why we hang the game to bleed. This is an old country custom going back many hundreds of years when small game such as rabbit/hare/grouse etc. were the only meal the poor man could afford. Very often when times were really hard, all parts of the game were eaten, and the skins used for other jobs and aids, and when they caught an abundance of food, they would use their surplus to barter for other things as with all game. Tie the rear legs (birds both legs) together and simply hang from any convenient hook, away from any predators, head downwards. This will make the game bleed, and in the case of the rabbit/hare the blood is very often used by the country folk in the making of gravy, and if you are fortunate enough to have a few drops of vinegar handy, place this in the container you intend to use for catching the blood. This will stop the blood from coagulating.

The word "paunched" simply means to remove the entrails, and clean and prepare the game accordingly.

## Skinning Methods

1. Hang the animal upside down, belly towards you. Allow to bleed in the normal way.
2. It is easier to skin an animal immediately after killing. Remove all entrails and skin soon as possible.
3. **COOK AS SOON AS POSSIBLE.**

**KEEP SKINS FOR AIDS**
Shoes, gloves, hats, etc.

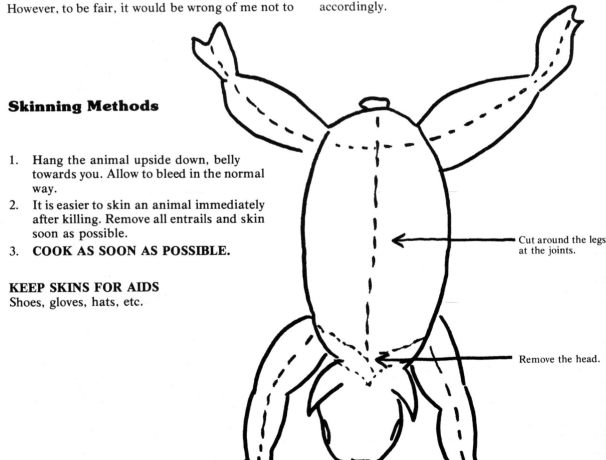

Cut around the legs at the joints.

Remove the head.

## Skinning a Hare or Rabbit

Lay the hare/rabbit on a large stone or log.

Chop off all the feet at the first joint.

Place your knife on the first joint and give a sharp tap with the butt of your hand.

Place your knife point just under the belly skin starting at the hind end.

Gently ease the skin away from the flesh around the hind end.

Push the legs through the skin until clear. Do this to both legs and also cut off the tail. Hold the rabbit by the hind legs and gently pull the skin down towards the head.

As before, ease the skin off the forelegs and pull over the head.

Keeping the hind end towards you, now put your knife point inside the rabbit's belly (not too deep) and cut towards the head until you reach the rib cage.

Put your hands inside now and remove all the entrails (do not throw away), the heart and kidneys are edible. Do not throw away the intestines, they can be used for baiting your traps.

Finally remove the head and rinse the whole game in clean water.

The game is now ready for cooking.

## Simple Methods of Catching and Skinning a Snake

Once again I stress that the only time one needs to actually kill snakes for food is under survival conditions. Of all the times that I have travelled I have never found the need to kill a snake without reason. A wave of a stick or a well aimed stone or lug soon has the snake scurrying off into the bush.

Remember, all species of snake are edible, and once you have learned the technique of trapping and skinning, all species can be done the same way, other than the Boa Constrictor. In this case the eating is the same, but trapping requires a little more thought and preparation. It is an exceptionally strong reptile and if captured alive requires very careful handling indeed.

An old American serviceman once told me that he never eats a snake that is dead. He always tries to remove the head while the snake is alive because someone once told him that this was one of the snake's ways of getting revenge. By this he meant that as soon as the snake was threatened in any way it injected itself with its own poison so that who or whatever ate it, would die. This, of course, is not true. So please, I beg you, never attempt to remove the head of a live snake unless you know what you are doing. Once removed, the head and the tail are of no use to you other than as bait.

It must be remembered though, that like all game you intend to eat, you must ensure that you gut and clean it well before cooking and eating.

While on the Zaire expedition I had the good fortune to be able to work with some of the world's top snake specialists, and they taught me many new and interesting things about the snake's habitat and food source. They also told me about the good and bad points of the snake family, its world-wide deployment, and how and from where it came. Some of these points I hope to be able to pass on to you in this book.

It is not important that you fully understand the snake's habitat, likes and dislikes, etc. but obviously, a little knowledge would not go amiss.

Nearly all snakes eat young birds, lizards, frogs and insects. All species are capable of crossing rivers and wide open spaces in search of food and shelter. Snakes are not generally territorial and indeed in most cases tend to live well together, in large colonies.

Like most wild animals the greatest threat to them is man. They will very quickly shy away from the presence of any human being. Occasionally though they will stand up and fight back if cornered; in particular the American Rattler and the far eastern Cobra. When suddenly surprised or cornered these species can be very dangerous indeed, so beware in the regions in which they live, especially if there are young around.

There are hundreds of species of snakes, some harmless and very shy; and some will attack if cornered, but in themselves are not dangerous. Others can kill by either injecting poison or crushing their victims. There are lots of mysteries surrounding snakes; their involvement in rituals, worship, killing powers, etc. and one of the most common ones is the eating of snakes and its dangers. Take it from me, snake is beautiful to eat and very simple to cook.

Again I think the best way to show you how to catch and cook a snake would be by the diagrams, which will also show you the simplest way to actually skin the snake once you have caught it. But please, please handle with care any snake you intend to eat, and never, never eat a snake that you have not caught personally, or have actually seen caught. There are exceptions to this of course, and that is when you are in the company of someone who you know to have been around a little and that the food that he is offering you is safe. Snake goes off very quickly, I found, so where possible try to cook all the snake as quickly as possible, even though you don't intend to eat it all there and then.

I find the taste of cooked snake not unlike that of a slightly salted chicken, and it is possible with a little careful planning to get more than one day's food supply from some of the even smaller snakes that are around.

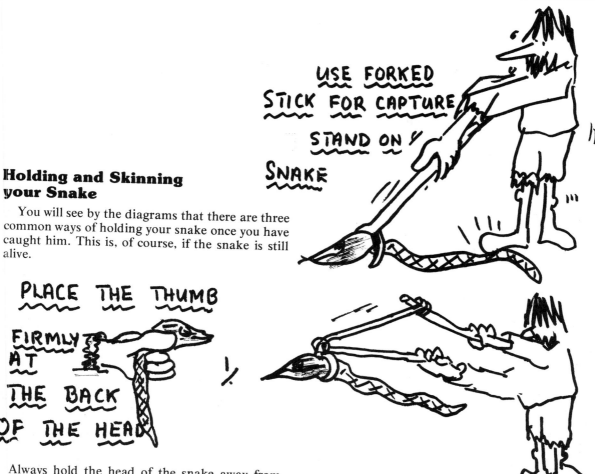

USE FORKED
STICK FOR CAPTURE
STAND ON
SNAKE

## Holding and Skinning your Snake

You will see by the diagrams that there are three common ways of holding your snake once you have caught him. This is, of course, if the snake is still alive.

PLACE THE THUMB

FIRMLY
AT
THE BACK
OF THE HEAD

Always hold the head of the snake away from you, and if possible at arm's length. Many a would-be survivor has found himself with a nasty bite on his face or wrist by incorrect handling. And while he has been busy holding the snake away from his body he has neglected to notice the body of the snake coiling around his lower limbs thus finding an anchor from which to strike. So beware. The safe answer, of course, is never to pick up the living snake anyway, unless transferring it to someone or something else.

THUMB

THREE FINGER
HOLD

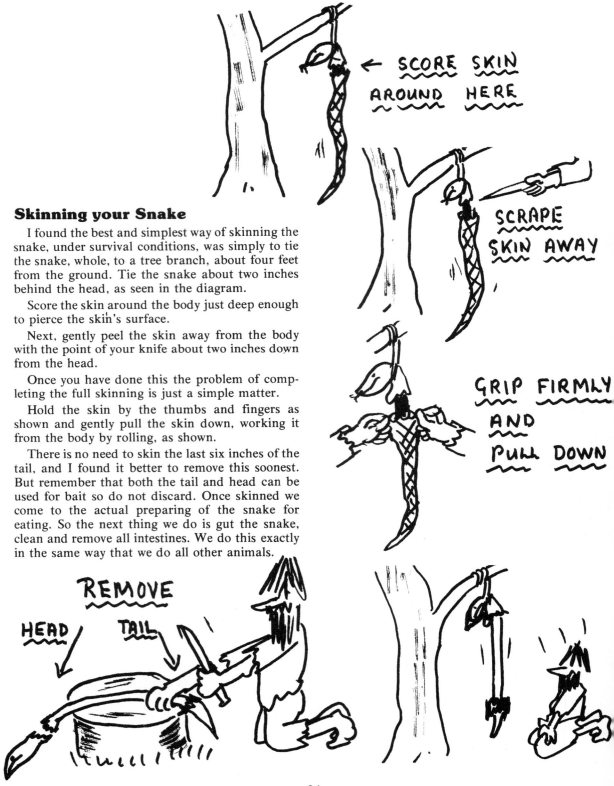

## Skinning your Snake

I found the best and simplest way of skinning the snake, under survival conditions, was simply to tie the snake, whole, to a tree branch, about four feet from the ground. Tie the snake about two inches behind the head, as seen in the diagram.

Score the skin around the body just deep enough to pierce the skin's surface.

Next, gently peel the skin away from the body with the point of your knife about two inches down from the head.

Once you have done this the problem of completing the full skinning is just a simple matter.

Hold the skin by the thumbs and fingers as shown and gently pull the skin down, working it from the body by rolling, as shown.

There is no need to skin the last six inches of the tail, and I found it better to remove this soonest. But remember that both the tail and head can be used for bait so do not discard. Once skinned we come to the actual preparing of the snake for eating. So the next thing we do is gut the snake, clean and remove all intestines. We do this exactly in the same way that we do all other animals.

SCORE SKIN AROUND HERE

SCRAPE SKIN AWAY

GRIP FIRMLY AND PULL DOWN

REMOVE

HEAD TAIL

## Skinning and Gutting the Snake

As soon as possible after the snake has been skinned correctly, we must set about gutting it. I found that the reptile meat seemed to go off very quickly once exposed to the light and air.

This is where the right kind of knife comes in handy, especially if it has a nice sharp point.

Once we have removed the head and the tail we can set about gutting the body. So place the snake on its back, head away from you. Insert the point of the knife but try not to pierce the intestines. Work the blade upwards, cutting open the snake's body.

Very gently, place your fingers inside and remove all the intestines and once again keep these for bait.

Open up the body wide and wash thoroughly. The snake is now ready for cooking.

You will have noticed at this stage that I have made no mention about the snake's poison sack. That is because if you have followed the directions in the diagrams correctly you should have removed all possible contact with the poison. For the snake to inject you with its poison it first must bite you with its two fangs and these must pierce the skin. The poison is then pushed down the fangs into your blood stream and begins its nasty work. However, if you do not remove the poison sack from the head and try to eat it you will simply transfer the poison sack from the snake to your own body, and I don't think there is any need to tell you what will happen to your stomach if you do this.

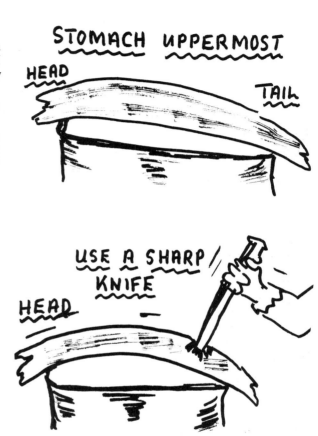

STOMACH UPPERMOST

HEAD

TAIL

USE A SHARP KNIFE

HEAD

REMOVE INTESTINES

## Curing and Smoking your Food

The golden rule of course:— Always gut and clean your food before attempting to cure it, be it fish or meat.

### The Plank Method

For this you will need a plank of wood large enough to pin your food to. An old log split into two makes and excellent backing for this.

Remember, curing is not cooking. All we are trying to do here is to seal in the juices so that we can use the food later on without it going off.

Place the plank in the upright position as shown, not too far from the fire which, incidentally, does not want to be too big. The idea is to seal in the juices slowly, without shrivelling the food away. Remember, embers give off the best heat.

If there is a strong wind blowing then you will have to put the plank down wind and close to the fire. You must remember to do both sides of the food to give it the full protection it needs. And if you want the food done quickly you must be on hand to see that it does not burn. If it is only smoking that you want to do then plenty of greens are needed to give off lots of smoke. Don't over do this as you will allow the smoke to go too deeply into the food and you will find it difficult to get the taste out even when you pre-cook the food. This is another of the survival skills that you need to practice at to become proficient.

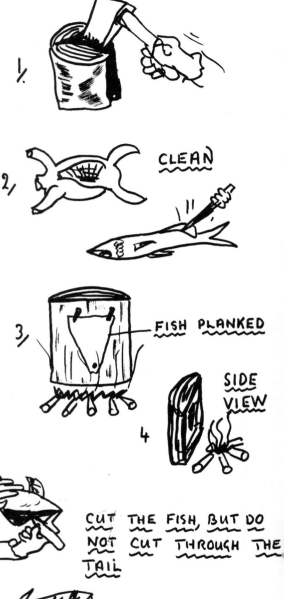

CLEAN

FISH PLANKED

SIDE VIEW

CUT THE FISH, BUT DO NOT CUT THROUGH THE TAIL

OPEN THE FISH OUT AND SCORE THE FLESH

HANG TO DRY OR SMOKE

# 4    Food, Water, Fire, Cooking.

## Fresh Drinking Water

Once, while serving in the Middle East and Cyprus, I was asked to undergo a survival exercise experiment which entailed living off pure oranges for fourteen days.

I agreed to do it on one condition and that was that the authorities gave me a week's leave afterwards to recover. They agreed and I was duly sent up into the Kyrenea mountains to a given location.

The first three days were to be my settling in time. This was to see if I had any allergies, too much vitamin C, etc. Well, everything went fine, and for the first three days once they had satisfied themselves that I was O.K. they left me alone, staying discreetly out of distance.

On the fourth day my urine and stools began to show a definite change in colour and the edges of my mouth, particularly the corners, began to get very sore. I mentioned this to the medics who took notes and saliva samples. At the beginning of the exercise they had not stipulated how much or how little of the oranges I could eat each day. That was left entirely to me. So, some days I ate just the flesh of the oranges while on other days only the juices.

The fifth day my stomach began to play up a little, and my movements became very irregular. By the sixth day my mouth was really beginning to feel sore, and tender, and I found that I now craved a little for fresh water or something else other than pure orange juice.

The seventh day, no change, but on the eighth I was really beginning to miss the water from my body now. Each day the medics had been re-assuring me that it was possible for the human body to go ten to twelve days without water, or any other liquids for that matter. By the evening of the eighth day I was really beginning to feel the pinch, and I must admit a little rough now. My whole body seemed to smell of oranges and I thought at the time that my skin was looking a little peculiar as well.

My scalp hurt and the inside of my throat was beginning to swell a little. At this stage the medics stepped in and told me that I should consider throwing in the towel.

On the morning of the tenth, my body had had enough and the medics thought so too, so I was taken off the project and admitted to one of the hospitals for observation. I had had nothing but pure orange juice and oranges for a full ten days, so I reckon my poor old inside had taken a rough ride. I recovered, but for two days they gave me nothing to eat but soup, and to help relieve the soreness on my lips, I had to suck slabs of margarine which would help they said, line my stomach, put some fats back into my inside, and help relieve the scalp ache which incidentally on the tenth day felt really sore.

The reason I have mentioned this story in this chapter is that many times I've picked up survival books where quite openly it claims that man can go for ten to twelve days without any liquids at all and from thirty to thirty-five days without food. Well, you can say I did not go without liquids for ten days, but I can say this that after the fourth day I craved fresh water and by the eighth day I was getting really desperate.

Now I always teach my pupils, no more than three days for you. If nothing else, all effort must be put into ensuring that you have at your disposal a source of fresh water when needed, for if you do not, in six days never mind ten, you will be too weak to make any effort to collect and you are going to need every drop when you do get some.

## Collecting Fresh Water

I stress the importance of finding fresh water. When I was very young I can remember going out into the Yorkshire Dales with my father and a friend of his who I now know to have been a poacher and being taught the basic test of finding out whether water is fit to drink or not by a simple wax test.

To test, all you had to do was to wriggle a finger in your ear and try to find some small particle of wax. With the other hand collect some of the water that you intend to sample either from some small puddle or stream, then place the finger with the wax into the water. If the water is clean and has no impurities i.e. chemicals, waste matter, etc, the bits of wax will float down to the bottom of the water in your hand. If the water is found to be contaminated, then the water surface will show a colour spectrum. By this I mean it will look as if you have poured some petrol or oil of sorts into the water in your hand.

Remember, this is only a quick, rough, survival guide. Without rigorous boiling and the correct use of chemicals, there is no easy way, or in fact safe way, of telling whether the water that you intend to drink is pure or not. Chemicals and boiling are the only safe way that I know of to kill off any bacteria or disease that may be present in the water.

If your body has been burned, or cut on the outside then you can deal with the injury fairly quickly. Unfortunately it is not possible to deal with any injury or disease that you may have picked up from the water until it actually starts to work on your body system; e.g. poisoning, upset tummy, diarrhoea, etc., etc.

## Methods of making Containers from Bark

A good survivor can, with just a little thought and practice, provide himself with all the necessary cooking utensils he needs from his natural surroundings.

For example, a flint hammer; rope from grass ovens from stones, or mud; containers from bark and many other useful things.

Let's take the water or food containers. These are not so difficult to make as one would think. Choosing the right type of bark, of course, is a must if you intend to use this method.

Birch bark is probably the best type of bark to use. It is very common in most countries, and easily recognisable. Choose a piece about eight to twelve inches long, preferably without any cracks or splits. If it feels very stiff do not try to bend it. Simply hold it over the fire for a couple of seconds. This will make it more pliable for you to work with.

The diagrams overleaf simplify the making methods for you so with a little patience, and practice, you will find yourself making many different kinds of containers.

One word of warning here though.

When it comes to the part where you have to lace up the sides in your containers try where possible to use the same type of bark as you are using on your containers. Small thin strands through very small holes will ensure a good water-tight seal. This, of course, must be if you are to use your containers to store water in.

## Fire

Every schoolboy knows that the Earth started from fire, or as we know it, volcanic matter. What schoolboys and indeed lots of adults do not appreciate is how the use of and methods of making fires have evolved over the many thousands of years.

Each time I go out on my lectures, I am invariably asked, "How many ways do you know of lighting a fire and how many can you do yourself?" I always give the same answer; if the conditions are right and the materials are there. For example, no matter how one tries to get a fire going with the use of the reflector glass, it is impossible if one does not have sufficient sun power to burn. By the same token, one can go on rubbing two sticks together all day and still not have any success if the wood is either wet or of the wrong type. We all know that friction eventually starts some form of smouldering, but we, as mere human beings, do not have the strength or stamina to maintain sufficient force to bring about this friction needed to start the fire. Fires can and indeed are started by the rubbing of two sticks together and from my experience I have found that the wood needs to be fully dry and at least one of the bits of wood needs to be of the hard variety. I have, at my home, 'light sticks' as I call them, which I have collected on my travels around the world, and I have spent many a happy hour with students on my courses watching them attempting to light a fire.

All this brings me to the point of stressing to the survivor just how important the ability to make a fire is, and more so the practice of always carrying around with you some means of starting a fire. Other than the actual rescue, there is no finer morale booster than having a good fire going in your camp. Your fire will provide you with all the comforts of home, both in protection and the building of aids.

The diagrams overleaf show, as I see it, the history of fire lighting from the past to the present.

## A Few Hints on Wood Burning

Remember, you can not cook on flames, only on embers. Flames burn your food, although they do boil water.

It simplifies things if you split your wood knowledge into two parts: Hard and Soft woods.

All soft woods are invariably resinous and burn fairly quickly; they are also very common and found in most parts of the world and are easily obtainable. They give off plenty of smoke, quick heat and very little embers, but are easy to cut.

Hard woods burn much more slowly and provide plenty of good embers. They are hard to cut and again common in most countries. This type of wood is normally placed on the fire the last thing at night to provide hot embers for the morning.

## The Tepee Fire

This method is probably the most common one used all over the world. Simple to light, providing there are plenty of dry materials available.

However, no matter how simple or practical it may be, this method will not work on snow or very wet ground. All fires, no matter which type, should always be built on some form of a platform. Because this method has no controlled fire surrounds it quickly consumes the fuels. More forest fires are started by this method than any other. Often the lazy campers just kick the fire out and move out leaving the fire to smoulder and relight.

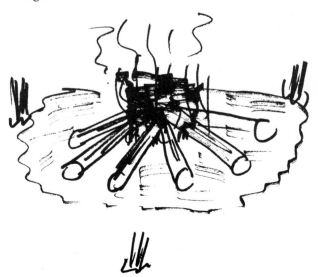

# HOW FIRES CAN BE STARTED

FIRE PLOUGH

HAND DRILL

PUMP DRILL

HANDBOW DRILL

STEEL AND FLINT

REFLECTOR GLASS

SULPHUR MATCHES

WIRE WOOL →

BATTERY

PETROL AND FLINT LIGHTER

ELECTRICAL

## The Fire

A difficult subject, not so easy to light as people think. It can be done, but it needs lots of practice without the correct fire lighting equipment.

**COOKING**
Hot Fire/Embers
Boiling Water

**BUILDING**
Drying, Mud
Making Stones
Hardening Wood-Metal

**CHARCOAL**
Embers Medicine
Filtration

**HAZARD**
Bone Splitting
Tent/Hydes/Basha
Clothing Burning

**WEAPONS**
Heating Metal for bending
Hardening/Wood
Game Sticks

**COMFORTS**
Warmth, drying
Morale. Heating Cave etc.

**SIGNALLING**
Smoke Light
Noise

**RELIGION ?**

**PROTECTION**
Ward off Animals/
Insects etc.

**MEDICINE**
Protection against
Frostbite/Cooking Herbs
Charcoal - Removing Lice
Leeches etc.
Boiling Water.

## The Platform Fire

All fires, irrespective of whether they are built in a trench, on snow, sand or stones, should always be built on a platform. This gives a good base to your fire. For the survivor this is an invaluable piece of information. On snow, for instance, try to build your platform of green wood.

The number of times I have seen people trying to light a fire tepee-fashion on snow, only to finish up with a wet soggy mess and in more than one case, use up all their matches trying and indeed nearly half a day in effort.

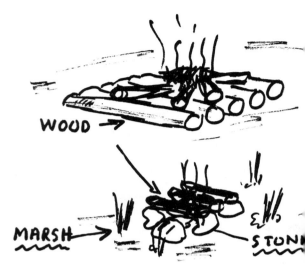

## Log or Pit Fires

Once you have built your fire on the platform, place good green logs around it. This helps to control the size of your fire and prevents spreading, containing all the embers inside the log area. It also stops you over-using your fuel.

Overnight campers normally use this method, needing hot embers in the morning for quick lighting.

## Stone Surround Fire

Simple, practical and nearly always available. However, many a novice camper has burned himself by incorrect handling of hot stones and in some cases been blinded or suffered serious facial injuries by stones taken from river beds which, once heated, have exploded. Good control is needed when using stones. Once heated they can be used to the campers' advantage; like using them as hot water bottles by placing them around your sleeping area. They can be used in your ground oven, they can be used for drying your kit on, etc. One very common cause of accidents with this type of fire is scalding. Trying to balance your cooking pots etc. on mis-shapen stones.

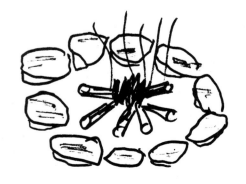

92

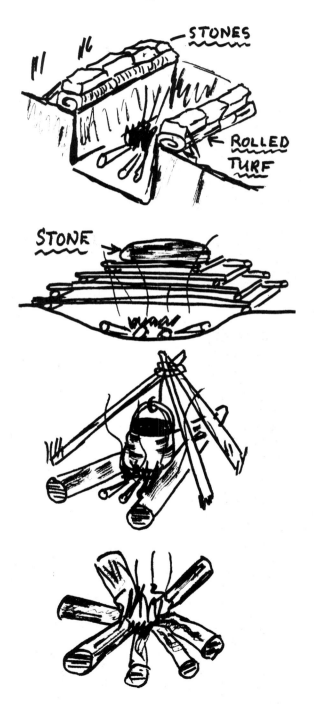

## The Small Pit Fire

Normally used by campers staying more than one or two days in one area.

The size of the pit regulates the amount of fuel you use. This method provides a good embers pit, and if need be, a good ground oven.

## Pyramid With Stone Fire

Provides a quick pile of embers, but if not controlled, quickly consumes large amounts of fuel. Controlled correctly, the stone weights down the fuel and simultaneously becomes hot. As the fuel burns down, down moves the stone, which can be used for cooking on. Use green wood at the top of the fire.

## A Trapper's Fire

Very common with group camping. Use only green or wet wood for side support. The logs provide a good support for an assortment of pots and pans. To cook efficiently this way, try to get as many embers as possible under the cooking pots. It is not necessary to build a pit between, but it is advisable to try to channel the wind between them. To do this, close together one end of the logs to about four inches apart, not the end away from the prevailing wind.

## The Indian Fire

This is a very good method for conserving fuel and labour, if the correct wood is used; thick green logs are best, as the ends nearest the fire dry out they smoulder. All the camper needs to do then is to push the logs together and just feed the fire with a little tinder each time.

When you settle down for the night push all the centres of the logs together, lay a couple of small green logs across them, then in the morning you will have a supply of good embers.

# ANIMAL DUNG FUEL BLOCKS

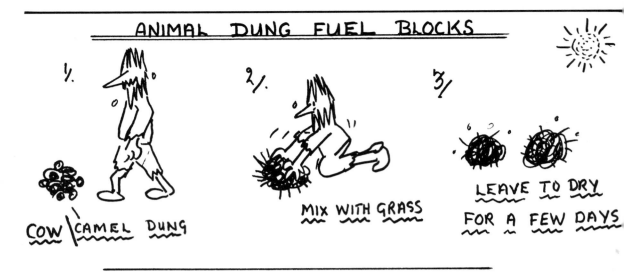

1. COW CAMEL DUNG

2. MIX WITH GRASS

3. LEAVE TO DRY FOR A FEW DAYS

4.

Sometimes the fuel for the fire that we urgently need is not available (mainly wood) so the survivor must turn again to improvisation skills.

Remember the rule for cooking. You need good hot embers to cook well, so your substitute fuels must, where possible, provide them.

Grass, for instance, is of no use at all in the making of embers, but used correctly on a fire, can help the survivor in many ways. For instance, wet grass makes heavy white smoke useful for signalling on moors or jungle terrain, while the ash from the grass makes excellent filtration powder for water purification and indeed poultices.

Grass used in improvising peat blocks also works very well. To make these blocks you will need fresh animal dung (the wetter the better), some green damp grass, a few twigs and of course, a fire or hot embers.

This method of making fuel for burning is still very widely used abroad even today, especially by desert people.

The making process may sound offensive and possibly crude, but I can assure you the end product is well worth it.

Making a few blocks is simple. Shape the fresh dung with the grass into a round ball. Ensure that it is well and truly mixed and in the European climate, place the ball near to a fire to dry out effectively. In desert regions, placing the ball on a hot stone in the sun will do just as well.

Once dried out the fuel can be stored ready for use as any ordinary peat block would be.

Alternatively, mix as before, place over hot embers, stick some of the twigs through as shown on the diagram. When you see the block drying out remove by the sticks.

Just before you go to sleep at night place one of these on the fire and you will be surprised and amazed at the amount of time it takes for one reasonably sized block to burn through.

## Some Methods of Cooking Your Meals

### Wrapping in Tinfoil

This is an excellent method if you are fortunate enough to have some available. The assets of the use of tinfoil are:

a.   You can use it again and again to cook in,

b.   You can preserve your food in it once you have cooked in it.

c.   You can carry your food around quite easily in the tinfoil even though it may be hot.

d.   By cooking in tinfoil you keep in all the natural goodness and, in most cases, prevent the meal from shrivelling up.

### Cooking in Mud

Normally used by the camper who stays in one place for more than a few days. A simple method, practical, easy to do and if done correctly will cook your meal excellently. Once you have learned to recognise a few edible herbs you can quite easily give your meal added flavours. Contrary to popular belief, you can cook any kind of meat by this method, especially if you place food in a ground oven.

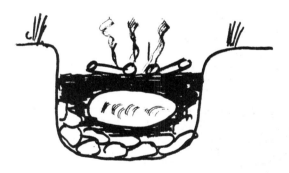

### Trench Fire Spit Roasting

Embers are a must here. When cooking, it is advisable to use two green sticks twisted together for the spit. When the animal gets hot it tends to keep swinging down. One of the drawbacks of this method is that it needs constant supervision and embers. Commonly used by campers all over the world. Slow, laborious, but effective.

Methods of how to prepare your food in these types of cookers are explained later on in the book along with diagrams.

## Seaweed

So that you can go out and gain confidence in the recognition and taste of seaweed, I've listed a few of the more common ones to be found locally. These are:

a. Laver

b. Knotted Wrack

c. Dulce

d. Carrageen (Irish Moss)

The water from boiled seaweed, especially Carrageen, makes an excellent throat gargle, while Dulce, with its very high iodine content, makes a very good bandage and poultice.

Some seaweeds are peculiar to certain countries, while others can only be found far out to sea, hundreds of miles away from shore.

Other species are often washed ashore by violent· storms and often give the survivor the wrong impression of natural habitat.

There are species that are only a couple of inches long, while others have been recorded at over twenty feet in length and while some of them can only grow in shallow waters, others can grow far out to sea at great depths.

It has been said that you can predict the weather from the handling of certain species of seaweed. On this I would not like to comment, for I certainly do not know how it is done.

Whenever you are dealing with salt water, take care. Excess in the body can be just as dangerous as too little. Should you find yourself in a situation where you are unable to get fresh water immediately, then never, never try to compensate by drinking sea water. This will only add to your thirst and dry you up more. If no water is available then you will probably have to revert to either drinking the blood of any fish that you may have been lucky enough to have caught, or from our old friend the turtle. But never raw seawater.

## Seafood

It is quite possible that the survivor may find himself surviving on the coast line. Well this is not so bad. At least the sea will offer up plenty of food in the way of fish, crabs etc, while the beach itself is full of surprises and is rich in survival aids and potential food.

Most beaches hold some form of seaweed and as every schoolboy knows, all seaweed is edible and non poisonous.

Seaweed is rich in minerals and in Vitamin C. However, special care must always be taken when picking seaweed. For eating purposes all seaweed must always be fresh and never try to re-use any that may be contaminated by being near sewers or any dead or decaying matter, seaweed spoils very quickly especially if left out in the sun for even a short while. A point worth mentioning here is that it is also very rich in iodine and has good medicinal qualities.

Seaweed can be boiled, eaten raw, or even used in soups. Quite often it has been used as a bandage and even as a poultice.

Always try to cook it in fresh water. This will help to remove the excess salt that it may be carrying, but more important, the water can be used as an insect repellant and a throat gargle.

Though I do not smoke myself, I have been with people who have dried it and smoked it in their pipes.

At this stage I would like to sound a note of caution and that is, beware of eating too much on an empty stomach. Though very nutritious it can also be very potent. My advice to you is, if you are genuinely interested in survival training, then go out and experiment. Once tasted you will never forget it.

Remember that some species of seaweed give off an irritant to both the throat and skin if not boiled first.

## Fishing Techniques

### The Lazy Fisherman

Stake driven into the sea bed when the tide has gone out.

When the fish is caught, you simply pull one end of the line through the hoop, this will move the other hook further out/it saves having to cast. This method is best used on the sea shore, but can be used in rivers and lakes if you can get a stake out far enough.

### BEER OR COKE BOTTLE ROD
### POLISHED STONE OR WOOD.

Force a stick through the bottle neck, twine the line around the bottle, weight and bait hook, cast out, the line will then run smoothly away.

## Fishing Skiffs and Platforms

It is possible, with a little practice and patience, to be able to put out three or four fishing skiffs to work for you, while you continue doing other things.

Many many years ago I was taught these methods by a professional poacher and, believe me, they do work.

If you're fortunate enough to have with you extra fish hooks or indeed line, then your luck's in.

Collect about half-a-dozen small sticks, preferably dry ones, about twelve inches long and about half an inch thick. Now follow the directions below.

1.   Tie four sticks together to form a platform as shown, two of them need to be about eight inches long. These are the uprights. Use either a grass rope or bark to bind them with.

2.   Now tie a cross member as shown. This needs to be fairly free and with at least two-thirds above the water. Onto this you can tie either a small piece of dry cloth or a leaf, as shown. This acts as your warning float.

3.   Tie a fish hook from either the centre pole, or from all or any of the float corners. The more hooks, the better the chances. Remember though, to hang the hooks at various heights. Once a fish is caught, it will attract others with its movements.

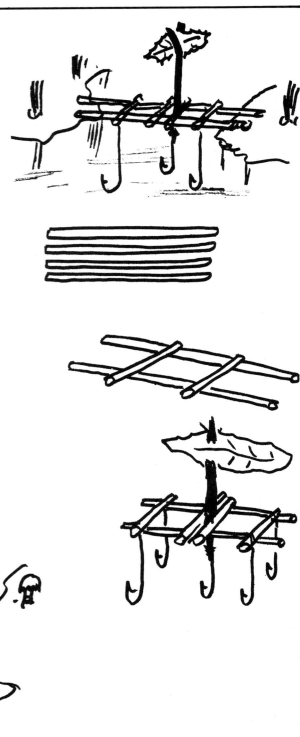

98

## Siting your Fishing Skiff or Platform

The siting of your skiff, or platform is very important if you need food quickly. I found the best method was to drive a stake into the river bed and allow the platform to float gently down-stream. If it is anchored correctly it will bob and weave around in the centre of the stream and once the platform comes to the end of its anchor rope, it will gently settle down and at this stage it will work best for you.

The slightest nibble or tug on the line will show by the rustling of the leaf on the centre pole. There is no need to wait around for the fish to bite, unless you feel that there are fish in the waters which eat others, which, of course, nearly all fish do.

You will find that the skiffs work best in gentle flowing waters, if possible about one hundred yards down-stream from any fast flowing rapids. This is also a very good place to put your fish basket or improvised fish net.

FLOATING SKIF

FISH BASKET

## Edible Sea Foods

As well as the many species of seaweeds, fish and turtles, etc., there is also a great abundance of fresh, rich, edible food to be had from the shell fish family of the sea. Below I have shown just a few of these. Some are very rich in protein and nutrients.

There is also a very considerable number of edible plants to be found around the shores. Some of these have the remarkable ability to be able to convert salt- to fresh-water just for the sole purpose of their own survival.

As I have said, all species of sea fish are not edible, so great care must be taken when choosing your food, especially the fish.

Some have poisonous spikes and fins, while others have poisonous flesh. Some species give off irritants to the throat and stomach and yet another species, the Electric Eel, can give off a very powerful shock when handled. Fortunately the good species far out-weigh the bad ones.

However, with a little patience and common sense you will come through, if you work at it.

## Cooking Fish in Fruit Juices

An excellent way of cooking your fish or meat when under survival conditions is, if you are lucky enough to have some fruit on hand i.e. plums, apples, pears etc., is to squash these into a container of sorts and collect the juice, put the juice into a cooking container and heat slowly. Place your fish, or meat into this having prepared it correctly first.

While the food is slowly cooking away, you can also make yourself a simple sauce to help make the food more palatable. For this you need some flours (fried rye grass heads or wild corn will do here) after it has been crushed and prepared correctly. You will also need some survival butter, again you can make this yourself quite easily from either cow or goat's milk. Mix the milk and the flour together into the hot fruit juices that you have just prepared your food in. Stir the milk and the flour first in a separate container before you put it into the cooking fat. At this stage it will form into a thick paste. Don't worry, once you put the butter into the juices it will dissolve almost immediately with stirring. After a short while, it will start to thicken again and at this stage the sauce is ready to eat. Simply pour it over your food, and soon you will find with a little practice you will become quite a *chef de cuisine*.

## Nothing Ventured — Nothing Gained

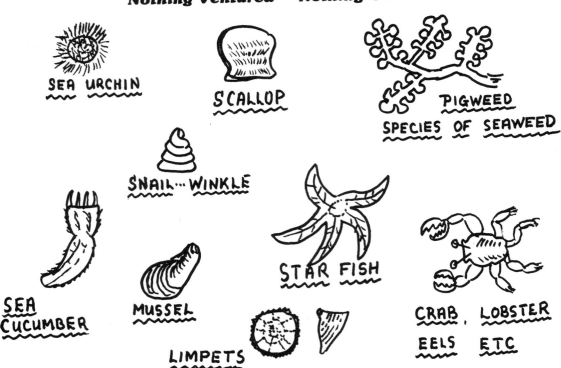

SEA URCHIN  SCALLOP  PIGWEED
SPECIES OF SEAWEED

SNAIL...WINKLE

SEA CUCUMBER  MUSSEL  STAR FISH

LIMPETS  CRAB. LOBSTER
EELS  ETC

# SOME DANGEROUS AND POISONOUS SEA FISH

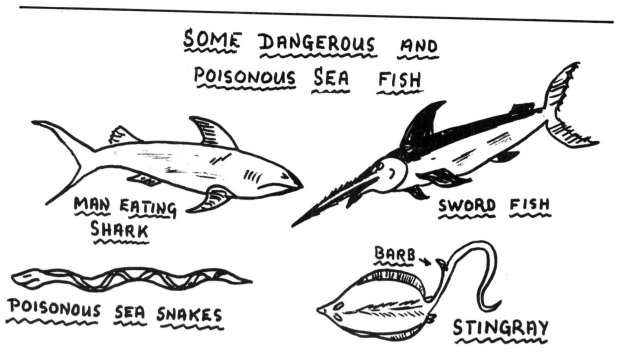

MAN EATING SHARK

SWORD FISH

BARB

STINGRAY

POISONOUS SEA SNAKES

PORCUPINE FISH

SCORPION FISH

MORAY EEL

JELLY-FISH

TOAD FISH

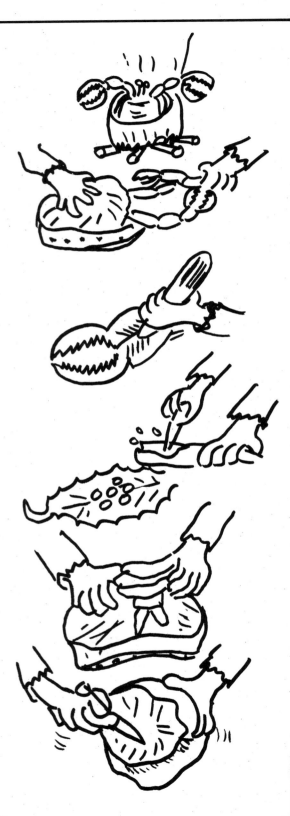

## Dressing a Crab that has been cooked (boiled)

a   After boiling your crab for fifteen to twenty minutes lay it on a stone or log. If you have no knife or scraper, collect an old cuttlefish or razor bill shell. These work fine for this job.

b   Twist and pull off the crab's legs and claws. Especially the two large ones.

c   Now remove the pincers and then crack open the claws with a small log or rock. (Edible meat)

d   .Remove as much meat as possible from the claws and legs into a container or a large leaf. (At this stage have something to cover the meat with, otherwise it soon goes off).

e   Next, place the crab on its back and very firmly pull the main body away from the shell. At this stage the stomach sack and other intestines will be visible. Save these for bait. (Not edible).

f   Now scrape out the soft brown meat from inside the shell case and collect. (Edible).

**WARNING:** Shell fish meat soon goes off. Eat as soon as you can after catching.

# Improvised Lobster or Fish Trap

ENTRANCE

**COMPLETED VIEW OF TRAP**

## How to make the trap

1 Cut and collect 20 to 30 lengths of tree twigs.
2 Use your boot or a large stone to form the trap shape.

BOOT OR STONE

CUT HERE

3 Tie up the ends of the twigs to form the trap as in the sketch above.
4 Cut the shape in half — remove the boot — make a circular lid, with a central entrance hole, and tie all together.

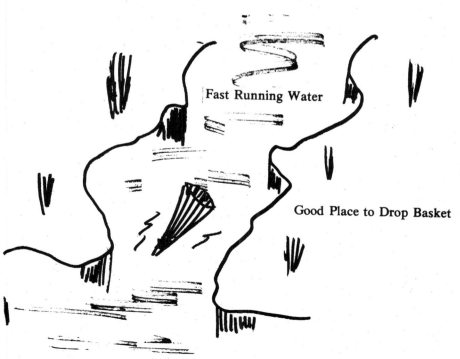

Fast Running Water

Good Place to Drop Basket

# TIDAL WATERS FISH TRAPS

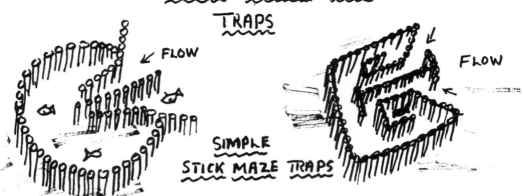

← FLOW

FLOW

SIMPLE STICK MAZE TRAPS

STONE WALL TRAP

LOG WALL TRAP

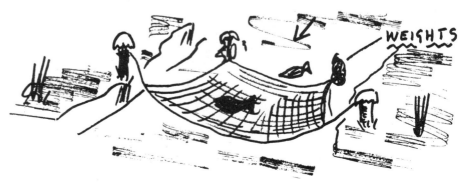

WEIGHTS

# Broken Bottle Fish Trap

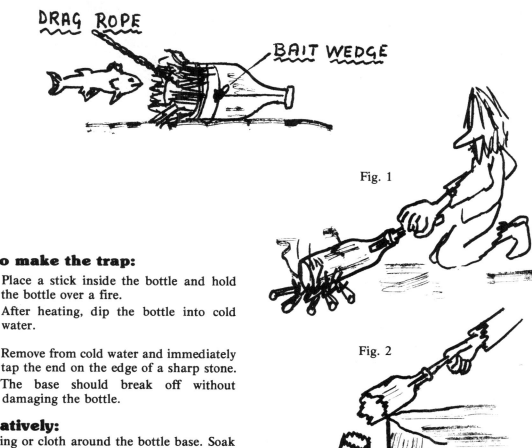

Fig. 1

Fig. 2

## How to make the trap:

Fig. 1: Place a stick inside the bottle and hold the bottle over a fire.

After heating, dip the bottle into cold water.

Fig. 2: Remove from cold water and immediately tap the end on the edge of a sharp stone. The base should break off without damaging the bottle.

## Alternatively:

Tie string or cloth around the bottle base. Soak in paraffin or petrol, and light. (Repeat as for Fig. 2.)

Keep the bottle base for use as: a cup, a night burner, a reflector.

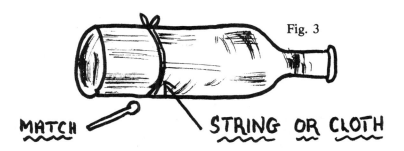

Fig. 3

MATCH          STRING OR CLOTH

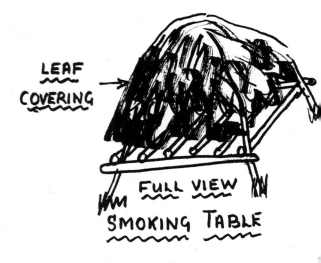

LEAF COVERING

FULL VIEW
SMOKING TABLE

## Smoking your Food

This method of curing is practiced all over the world, not only for everyday living but also for gain.

Once again the food is not cooked by this method, but is simply smoked, giving a carbon covering to the food to protect it.

It is possible, by placing certain herbs on the food, to actually smoke the flavours of the herbs into it.

Make yourself a smoking table as shown in the diagrams.

To get the best from this method it helps if the smoke is kept constantly around the food. By this I mean enclosed.

**Warning:** Always use wood for curing. Never, never try to do it with chemicals, tar, or coal. Not only is this very dangerous to your health, but you will completely spoil any chances of using the food later on.

If possible hang the food up so that the smoke can get all the way round it at once.

The longer you leave the food in the smoke the deeper the smell goes into the food.

Slow heat and smoke will give you long lasting protection, whilst quick smoking gives you only a couple of days. But in both cases the food will have a hygienic cover of carbon which is what we were after anyway.

Remember, fish of any description, unless treated immediately, will quickly go off; in some cases within the hour.

LIGHT LEAF COVERING.

OPEN VIEW

OPEN PLAN SHOWING
HOW TO HANG THE FOOD

106

## Fishing with a Balloon or Plastic Bag and Net

Firstly improvise your net; then blow up the balloon or plastic bag, tying it firmly. Place the home-made net over the balloon/bag and attach as many fishing hooks to it as you need.

Do not forget to put on your anchor line, preferably one on each side as shown in the diagram.

This is another excellent method of improvisation and you will be amazed just how effective it can be.

How it works:— The bag or balloon of air acts just like your fishing rod action. As the fish tug on the bait the bag will be pulled down under the water, then as the buoyancy takes over it pops back up again, snatching the fish and like the fishing skiff, as one hook attaches then the movement of the captured fish attracts others. I first saw this method being used in the Congo Basin in Africa, only there they were using gourds hollowed out which were strung across the river. I've even used a more modern method myself, using a blown up contraceptive. You may smile, but when on survival 'nothing ventured, nothing gained' and my net was an old pair of ladies tights from which I hung the hooks.

## Turtles' Eggs

Turtles lay eggs, in large clutches. To do this they go ashore in the moonlight.

Once ashore they move with caution to the selected hatching place and as soon as they arrive they start a very loud hissing noise to frighten off anything that may be around to disturb them.

The female turtle digs a hole in the soft sand with her flippers to a depth of about eighteen inches to two feet. This is done very rapidly, taking about ten to fifteen minutes.

The turtle now lays her eggs in the hole, covering each layer with sand. They generally lay about 150 to 200 eggs in about twenty to thirty minutes. Once the eggs have been laid the turtle scoops the remaining sand back over the nest and smooths it out in such a way that few people, on seeing the spot, would guess what was there.

Once the whole process has been completed without any waste of time, the turtle makes its way back to the sea, leaving the eggs to be hatched by the heat of the sun. During the season each female turtle lays three clutches of eggs, at intervals of a fortnight to three weeks.

Directly the young are hatched they fall victim to many predators, and immediately after birth they begin to make their way to the sea where once again, they fall victim to the sea's predators.

The turtle's eggs are edible and very tasty. About the size of a tennis ball, they can be eaten raw or cooked just like an ordinary egg.

The flesh of the turtle is very tasty when cooked and there have been cases on record where survivors have been known to drink the blood, and eat the flesh raw. For myself, I found the best results were in cooking the meat in leaves and mud.

## Edible Foods

The ever popular banana, of course, needs very little explanation, though there are one or two methods of cooking it that one does not usually see in this part of the world.

Here we are used to seeing the banana in big bunches on the stalls and the only method of eating that most people know is the plain simple peeling and eating direct. There are about half-a-dozen species of banana from the big yellow one down to the little red sugar one found in Africa. Bananas can be eaten raw, cooked in leaves, cooked on a stick as a kebab or mashed up and used in the making of bread. There is also a species that is very starchy and needs to be well cooked before it is eaten.

BANANAS

The Mango is another popular fruit and grows all over the tropics. The tree grows very tall; well into the thirty to forty feet region. The fruit at first appears as hard green balls and as they ripen they turn into a soft reddish-green fruit. At this stage they are deliciously sweet and very soothing to the palate. A fruit that I strongly recommend that you try as soon as you are able.

The following are a few of the common edible foods that one could expect to find when travelling the jungles. Not all foods in the jungle are edible uncooked. Some have to be well cooked to remove some of the various poisons that one can find.

**Tapioca** known as Manioc or Cassava. A tall, shrubby plant growing about ten feet high. The leaves and the tubers are edible though caution must be used when choosing the right one. Both are edible but one needs to be well cooked to remove the hydrocyanic acid. In the case of the bitter one, once boiled, squeeze the tubers well and remove all the moisture. Then if you wish you can either eat the food raw or bake it into small cakes.

EDIBLE LEAVES

EDIBLE TUBERS

**Coconuts.** Not only an excellent source of food but also a very good supply of drinking water as well. The nut kernel inside the hard, rough casing is a very nourishing food and can either be eaten raw or cooked and when pulped, the oil from the kernel makes excellent cooking oil. The outer casing, of course, makes a very good water container.

The oils from the coconut provide the survivor with a means of protection from sun burn. The base of the leaves also provide another excellent source of food not unlike cabbage when boiled. It can, of course, be eaten raw. The nuts may seem a little hard to open at first sight, but simply bash it on a good sharp rock, or a pointed stake driven into the ground, and you will soon have it open.

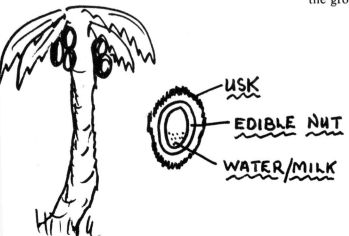

USK

EDIBLE NUT

WATER/MILK

STAKE

## A Water Container from a Log

Another very simple method of making a water boiling container is from an old tree log. Try to choose a hard wood, if possible. These seem to have less resin in them than the soft ones, though I must admit that they are harder to scoop out.

It needs to be about twelve inches long by about six inches across.

Remove the top section leaving about two thirds of the log, that is if you are lucky enough to have an axe with you.

Hollow out gently as if you were making a small dug-out canoe (be careful not to split the sides at this point).

When you reach the depth you require, remove all the remaining splinters and, if possible, try to smooth out the inside, though this is not absolutely necessary.

The log is now ready to use. Place it by the side of your fire (not in it). You may find, at this stage, that you will have to support the log to prevent it from rolling. The next thing now is to remove some small stones from the fire and place them in the container to boil the water.

It will surprise you how quickly the water will boil by this method. Another good thing about this method is that any dirt or scum that may be in the container will cling to the stones. You can also leave your water in the container overnight. This will help to swell the wood, and stop it from cracking.

**WARNING:** Trees like the Yew, Holly, Laburnum Rhododendron and Privet give off poison saps.

## DO NOT USE.

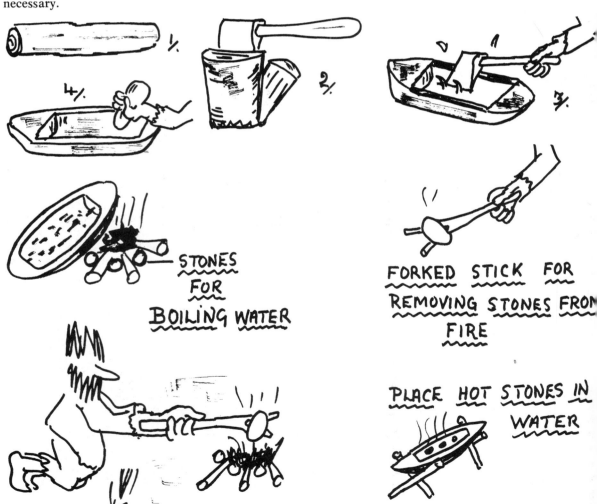

STONES FOR BOILING WATER

FORKED STICK FOR REMOVING STONES FROM FIRE

PLACE HOT STONES IN WATER

It is very important to your survival diet that you try to vary it a little, if you find that you may have to stay a while in one area.

So I have jotted down a few well tested recipes I know:

The ever-popular potato. Everyone knows how to make chips. Even in Malaya I found the jungle people making chips as we do. They peel the potato, cut it into strips and drop it into the cooking fat. The only difference between us is that we tend to cook ours in vegetable oils, while they use animal oil.

Cooking potatoes in mud is another excellent method widely used. This is the same principle as the pressure cooker and I might add it seems to me to give the potatoes a much nicer taste.

Try cooking your potato along with any bits of meat that you may have spare. By this I simply mean, place some potatoes on the end of a stick along with some bits of meat and hold them over the fire for a while until cooked. Once again you will be surprised at just how delicious they taste; I have done this many times with rabbit for my meat.

Mash some potato with an egg, some flour, if you have any available, some diced meat and mushrooms. Mix well and then roll out into hamburger cakes. Place these on a hot stone and cook until nice and brown. You will not only find these delicious to eat, but they are easy to carry round with you should you suddenly have to make a fast exit from campsite.

It is not a bad thing for the would-be survivor to attempt the common homely dumpling. They are not nearly as hard to make as one would think. For survival dumplings all you need is some flour, a pinch of salt (though not altogether necessary) a drop of milk and a couple of fresh eggs. Mix well together, add a little water, roll out into paste, then drop them into your stew.

## Eggs

All eggs are edible, some tastier than others, of course. But under survival conditions, should you be lucky enough to come across any (fresh) then eat them. Do not worry about conservationists here, (life before pleasure). I am sure thay would not object anyway.

1. *BOILING* No problem here, we need:
   a. a container of sorts
   b. a fire and of course, water.

Any old tin will do, or indeed paper bag, or hollowed out log, as I have already explained under 'Types of Fire' chapter. How to boil water in a log, paper bag and bark kettle. There is no need here for me to cover it again.

2. *POACHING* As above but now the egg is broken open and placed in the water to poach. At first this will seem un-natural and messy but do not worry, you will be amazed how quickly it does poach.

3. *SCRAMBLED* On a hot flat stone, or flat piece of metal is probably the simplest to practice. At first you may seem to be losing much of the egg by burning and running but again do not worry, once you start to pull it all together it soon takes shape and smells delicious.

111

# Methods of Cooking

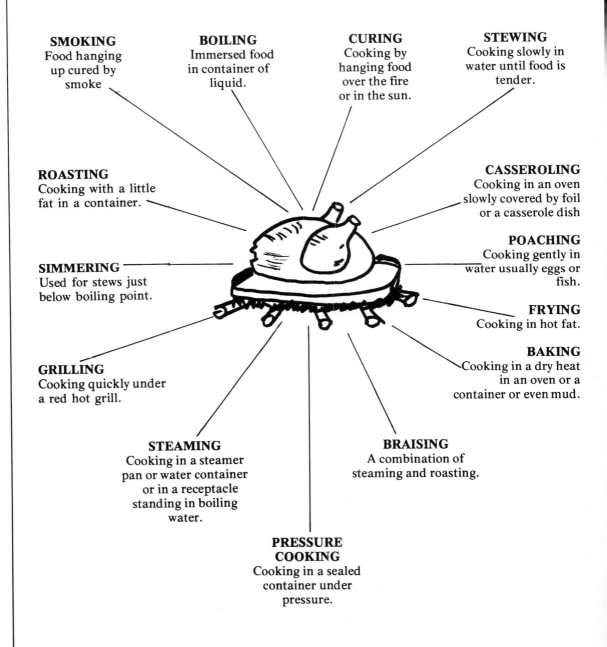

**SMOKING**
Food hanging
up cured by
smoke

**BOILING**
Immersed food
in container of
liquid.

**CURING**
Cooking by
hanging food
over the fire
or in the sun.

**STEWING**
Cooking slowly in
water until food is
tender.

**ROASTING**
Cooking with a little
fat in a container.

**CASSEROLING**
Cooking in an oven
slowly covered by foil
or a casserole dish

**POACHING**
Cooking gently in
water usually eggs or
fish.

**SIMMERING**
Used for stews just
below boiling point.

**FRYING**
Cooking in hot fat.

**GRILLING**
Cooking quickly under
a red hot grill.

**BAKING**
Cooking in a dry heat
in an oven or a
container or even mud.

**STEAMING**
Cooking in a steamer
pan or water container
or in a receptacle
standing in boiling
water.

**BRAISING**
A combination of
steaming and roasting.

**PRESSURE
COOKING**
Cooking in a sealed
container under
pressure.

## Try These

### Poached Crisp

Take a small Elderberry stem with flowers attached from a fresh young tree.

Dip the flower end into your pot of hot cooking fat. Shake it out and hold over the embers of your fire (not flames). After a couple of minutes it will be cooked nice and crisp and ready to eat. Fat from any animal or nuts will do fine.

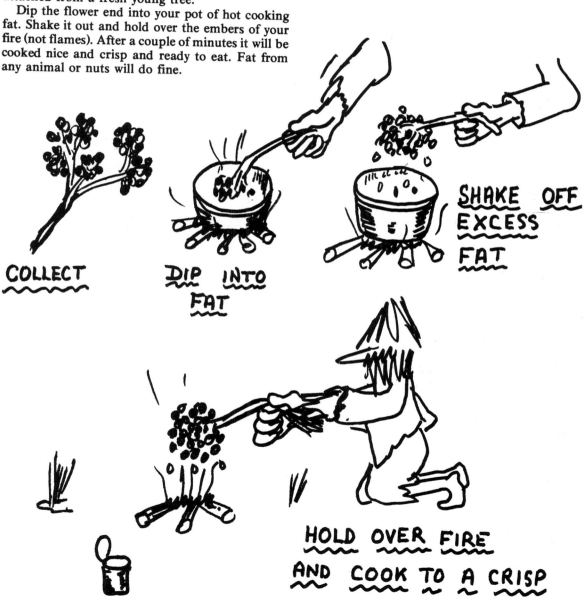

COLLECT

DIP INTO FAT

SHAKE OFF EXCESS FAT

HOLD OVER FIRE AND COOK TO A CRISP

## Try These

### The Sun Flower

1. Collect a good supply of fresh sunflower heads.

2. Remove all stems and petals. Place the centre sections in your container with a drop of hot water.

3. Make a good wooden or stone crusher and pound the seeds into a pulp.

**CONTAINER**

4. Do not worry about the gooey mess and there is no need to filter (though you can if you wish). In its pulp form it is now ready for cooking being an excellent natural oil with a beautiful refreshing taste.

**COOK**

**SCRAPE OUT AND USE**

114

## Survival Cake Recipe

**INGREDIENTS:**
1. **Any of the following:**
   **Hazel Nuts**
   **Big Nuts**
   **Acorns**
   **Conkers**

2. **Mixed with any or all of the following:**
   **Dried Elderberry**
   **Blackberry**
   **Sloeberry**

3. **Mashed with either:**
   **Crushed corn/wheat**
   **Willow grass heads**
   **Rye grass heads**
   **Elder flower heads**

Mix the chosen ingredients well, adding water to form a dough. Form the dough into a long thin strip and wrap around a clean green stick. (Form a sort of helter-skelter effect). Bake the bread over a hot fire, embers preferably, until a light crispy brown.

This can be eaten warm or wrapped up and saved for the next few days.

## Try These

1.  Take the bottom section from a bunch of fresh marsh reed.

2.  Open the stem and remove the white core.

3.  Take the ears from a bunch of fresh wild rye grass or corn.

RYE GRASS

CORN

4.  Mix both together with water or crushed berries.

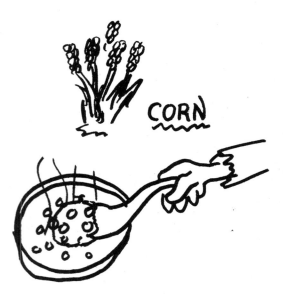

5.  Once made into a paste place on a hot container on your oven on hot stone and cook like a biscuit.

SURVIVAL BISCUITS

## An improvised water container from Birch Bark

Remove a good sized piece of Silver Birch bark (ensure no holes or cracks)

It needs to be about twelve to fourteen inches square.

Using a forked stick, gently warm over the embers of your fire. This will allow the bark to bend more easily when you come to start folding.

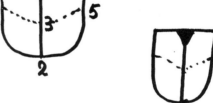

While it is still warm, mark your shape and gently score as shown in the diagram. This will ease the folding. Now make a small 'V' cut where Fig. 1 is shown. Fold firstly 1 to 2 as shown, then 3 to 4.

After your first fold you should end up like this——

Gently now push in the Fig. 3. 4. 5. Your container should now start looking like the one shown here———————————————————

When completed you can support your container as shown by simply using a piece of your bark string and lacing your stick to the cup, try though to use only very thin bark string, and preferably the same bark.

117

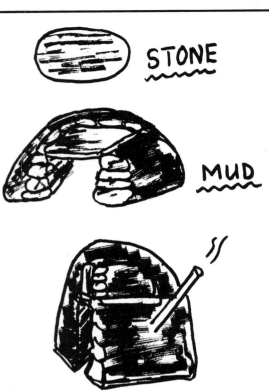

STONE

MUD

SIDE VIEW SHOWING CHIMNEY SECTION

## Building an Oven from Mud

Find yourself a large round stone about a foot in diameter and fairly smooth.

Prepare the bottom half of the oven now. For this you will need a large flat stone for the oven base. It is important that it goes in at this stage.

Cover the stones with the mud or clay that you have prepared and ensure that you cover the stones well. There is no need to cover the inside of the fire grate. You must ensure that you put a chimney in and for this you will need a stick about four feet long and about two inches thick.

Once you have made the bottom half of the oven, place the large round stone on the oven bed as shown. Cover the whole stone with mud, except the oven entrance. Wait until it begins to dry out a little then gently turn the stone making the inside smooth. Remove the stone and finish the smoothing out inside with your hand. The oven is now ready for use. I would advise you at this **stage** to start with a little fire, until the oven has had a chance to dry out slowly. Don't forget also to give the chimney stick a couple of twists before you remove it, again smoothing the inside.

FRONT VIEW SHOWING OVEN COMPLETED

SIDE
VIEW

STONE

## Improvised Cooking Pans

To make the correct use of this type of cooking it is advisable to make an open type fire, as shown on the sketch. Collect a reasonably large, flat stone, about twelve inches across. Place this on the fire pit as shown. Ensure that this stone has not been taken from a river bed, or soaked in a bog or any wet place. If too much water has got into the stone then when it gets hot, it can easily explode in your face.

Another simple method of cooking is to try to get hold of an old tin can, open it up as shown and beat it into shape to make a simple frying pan. Attach a modified handle of sorts and you are away.

In the cooking chapter I explain just how simple it is to make rough bread cakes.

Once you have learned to recognise various herbs then you can start adding colour and taste to your meals.

## Cooking

Another excellent method of cooking your meal uses boiling mud, mixed with grass or reeds. Make yourself a hay box from logs and packed straw. Dig a hole deep enough in the ground to accommodate the box and if possible make a lid, as tight a fit as possible, that can be quickly removed. Once the box is made and the mud and grass have boiled well, wrap your meal either in large leaves or in polythene, place this in the box and cover it well with the boiling mud and grass. Make sure that it is all well and truly covered, place the lid on it and leave it for a couple of hours.

This method works exactly the same way as a pressure cooker and it normally takes about two hours to do a fair-sized fish or chicken leg. But, to get the best results from the hay box, it is best if you can pre-cook your meal before placing it inside.

HAY PACKED TIGHTLY

BOILED MUD AND GRASS

GRASS

LEAF

MUD

To store your food and keep it cool and fresh, place it in a polythene bag, if you are lucky enough to have one handy and suspend in water. But first, tie up the end and make sure that it has no leaks and also tie a suspension rope on to the bag so that you can pull it out of the water when you require it.

FOOD SUBMERGED IN A PROTECTIVE BAG

HAVE NO FEAR FOR THIS PRESSURE COOKER WILL NOT BLOW UP IN YOUR FACE

## Try This

## Improvised Pressure Cooker

1. Build a reasonably sized fire, with plenty of hot embers.

2. Get a good green stake, or if possible a piece of metal tube of sorts.

3. You will need a tin for the next move. A large bean tin would be ideal.

4. Clear the centre of the fire and put a few stones in as shown.

Put the stick into the centre and put your food on the spike. Dig the stake in and place the can over the top.

5. Tie plenty of grass around the tin and light. This will burn quickly and make the food inside sweat. The heat from the fire will keep the steam inside the can going and this works on a pressure cooker system.

## Herbal Recognition

I have left this subject until the last, because I feel that this is a very complex one. Though one can easily purchase a good cheap book on this subject, for actual physical experience one needs to go out and recognise herbs on sight to gain real confidence.

For many years now I have been studying the medicinal and food value of herbs for use on my survival courses and one of my favourite parts on the course is to take my students on what I call my walk-about. For gaining first-hand knowledge and confidence I feel this is an excellent way of teaching. On these walks they can actually see, feel and often taste the herbs. Those we cannot taste on sight we take back to prepare at the centre.

There is a lot of folk-lore attached to the herbalist world. In the old days it was always the man who went out to farm, whilst the women stayed at home preparing the food. This very often meant the use of herbs for the flavouring of the meals and because the women had to travel around looking for the various herbs, collect them and prepare them in their own cooking pots it is probably because of this that some women were suspected as witches. I think it would be fair to say that many of these so-called witches were killed off in this way. So sadly a vast amount of first-hand practical knowledge has been lost. When one looks at the very old herbal books, very few, if any, are written by women. Today however, with modern cooking techniques and the vast amount of public eating places there is a great demand for the use of herbs in the never-ending demand for foreign dishes that the public want and most of the books written today are by women who specialise in cuisine.

LEARN TO RECOGNISE

## Fungi

The nutritional value of certain species of fungi is very high indeed. Fungi contain protein, more so than vegetables and in some cases contain a large amount of fats.

The calorific value of fungi is also very good, the Boleti family in particular. Fungi contain a certain amount of phosphorus and in some cases a high degree of vitamins.

For confidence in the tasting and recognition of fungi all I can advise you to do, at this stage, is to learn to recognise a few of the more common ones and taste them.

Also make a point of recognising the more common deadly species. Not only from books, but by actually going out and trying to physically find them. By doing this, not only will confidence grow in recognition, but you will also be surprised how quickly your knowledge of the growing habits of fungi will improve. Also which animals feed on them.

Fungi used as food and indeed as medicines have been mentioned as far back as biblical times and probably the most prolific time when fungi were used for food was in the early twelfth and thirteenth centuries.

Once, in the Middle East, I saw an arab treating a wound by applying a fungi poultice and on returning to this country I made straight for my local library and some reading. I had heard that certain stables used certain species of fungi to cure ills of horses but never man. Some of the medieval reading I did astounded me.

The Romans, it seems, were great believers in cures from certain fungi and boiled fungi poultices were in great demand as an eye cure.

## Mushroom and Fungi Recognition

I am often asked, "What is the difference between fungi and mushrooms?" Well, without trying to split hairs, I think the best answer is, none. A fungi specialist I know tells me that mushroom is an old English name for fungi, while another says, anything that grows up from the ground is a mushroom and species that grow from trees and lie on walls are best classed as fungi. So, to keep the book straight, mushroom and fungi are one.

It is estimated that in England alone there are about 3,000 species, varying in size from the microscopic yeast to the Great British common earthball. Both species are edible.

The peculiarity of fungi is that though they grow from rotten vegetation and mainly from the ground, unlike other plants, they have no pigment or chlorophyll, which is necessary to give the green colouring that is common in other land plants.

Not all fungi are poisonous, though some certainly are. There are lots of superstitions and myths attached to the fungi world. Most of these, of course, are nothing more than old wives' tales, but it would be fair to say that from some of these, handed down through the generations, some very useful information has been gained.

Some species of fungi are very rich in protein and other species help us in the medical world.

It is not my aim to go too deeply into the evolution and chemical make-up of the fungi. Should you want to go deeper, then there are some excellent books on the market that will give you all the information you need to know.

## Fungi Recognition

I have chosen to talk about a few fungi only, for it would be impossible to cover all of them in this book. For my own purposes I have found that I need to know about 20 which grow in this country. Though I have made a point of acquainting myself with over two dozen of the poisonous variety, when I go overseas to somewhere new I leave fungi well alone unless I am with a local expert.

Let's glance at three of the more common fungi found in Europe. Their recognition will give you confidence and encourage you to find out more on your own initiative. There is for instance the Amanita Phalloides, or Death Cap, which, as its name suggests, is deadly poison.

It has a characteristic cap about 4 to 15 cm. across, coloured in varying shades of green, merging into slate grey. Fully grown it is four to five inches tall, standing in groups of three or four. In its mature state it has white and green patches on the stem, and a recognisable "ring" which hangs down just under the cap. It is also bulb shaped at its base.

It tastes like hay and smells like clover. Its spores are white and it grows in all types of woods, from early spring to winter. There is no known antidote and even when boiled for long periods it does not become harmless, let alone nourishing! Symptoms of poisoning by this fungus can appear as late as two days after consumption. This raises an important point for the survivor: always try to remember what you have eaten, so that if you fall ill when rescued you will be able to tell the medics.

## Amanita Muscaria (Phalliodes family) Poisonous

This fungus has a colour ranging from bright red to orange red. It has a globular cap merging into a disc shape. The red area has white spots which turn into "warts". The stem is white with greying streaks. Like the Amanita it has a ring formation but instead of the large "bulbus" its stem thickens.

The spores are white, and the fungus grows in the autumn in most woods, but especially under birches, firs and larch, open to the light.

Though the flavour is agreeable it is deadly poison.

**Amanita Virosa** — Same family as the above and also poisonous. It has a white, globular cap, with dark tint in the centre. It has an oily appearance in humid weather and glossy in dry weather. It has the characteristic "skirt" hanging down and a stem with white scales.

The flavour is disgusting and should not be eaten. Boiling does not help and a small quantity — 20 grams — is sufficient to kill.

WHITE WARTS

RED CAP

WHITE
SCALES

SCALEY
BULBUS

SLIMY
WHITE
CAP

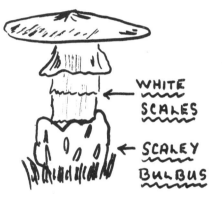

WHITE
SCALES

SCALEY
BULBUS

SKIRT

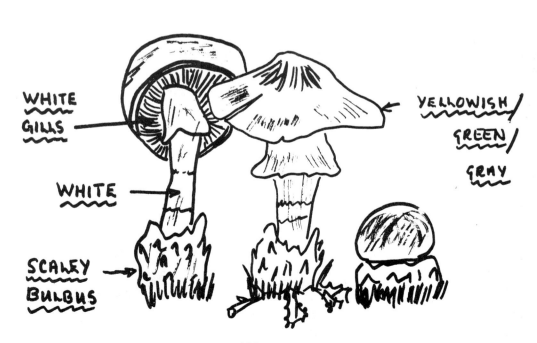

WHITE
GILLS

WHITE

SCALEY
BULBUS

YELLOWISH/
GREEN/
GRAY

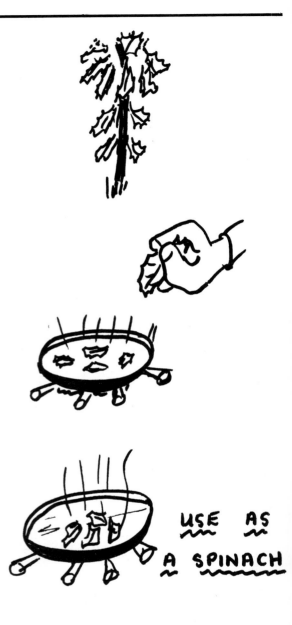

## The Nettle (Urtica Dioica)

1. Found in European countries, widespread and abundant.

2. Season: all year round. Flowers June/Sept. Nutritional value: High.

A. Preparation: Remove fresh young leaves and shoots from the stinging nettle plant. Preferably before flowering starts (see above).

B. When you have collected a good supply place them in water and boil.

C. At this stage the sting poison will disappear and the water in the pot will turn a dark murky green. Do not discard.

D. The leaves are now ready for eating in salad form, when cold, or as a hot vegetable, though at this stage you will probably need some form of additive to remove bitter taste if you are not used to them.

E. The water can be used as a form of soup, but again it will be exceptionally bitter.

F. The water makes an excellent hair shampoo.

G. The roots are edible but must be well soaked and roasted before eating.

H. The stems when stripped of leaves, crushed and placed in hot water can be broken down into very fine and very strong rope/or fishing line (see Making Rope).

## DRIED NETTLES MAKE EXCELLENT ROPE

Another excellent use for the nettle is its use in making rope and first class rope it makes as well.

Firstly you collect yourself a large bundle of fresh long nettle. Strip off all the leaves and place them on a flat surface. If you are lucky enough to have a container of sorts long enough to be able to place the stems in then fine, because the next move is very important. In your container put some hot water, place the stems in and leave to soak for a while. Hot water is better, and gives quicker results but no matter if you don't have a container then you will have to do with treading the stems in some stream or puddle. Once the water process has been completed. In the case of the hot water treatment about two hours, the stream leave for a day.

Take the stems out and lie on the flat surface to drain off. But while the draining process is working, grab a nice smooth round stone and very gently beat the nettles, squashing the water from them.

The next process is to hang the nettles out to dry over a bar as shown. While the nettles are drying we now have to make ourselves a thread comb. For this all we need is a small log about twelve inches long and into it we have to bang some spikes to form the comb. Again the diagram explains.

Once the fibres have dried the next move is to pull them through the comb to split them down into even finer fibres. Work gently but ensure that the fibres do not get wet again at this stage.

The fibres are now ready for spinning. If you wanted to you could form some rough field dye from boiling herbs, but once again you would have to ensure that the fibres were properly dried before you could use them again for rope or weaving.

The diagrams explain again for you.

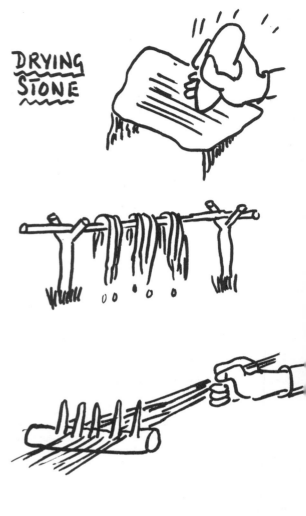

DRYING STONE

## Nettle Twine and Rope Making

Collect a good pile of fresh nettles and remove all the leaves.

If you have a container to boil the nettles in, fine. If not, not to worry, you will have to find some small stream or puddle and do a bit of trampling to help break down the stems.

Once soaked you will need a flat surface to be able to beat out the nettle and let the water dry off. You will also need something to crush the stems with. At this stage a flat stone or log will do.

When you have crushed the stems they must be left to dry off naturally and while this is going on you will need to build some form of drying rack. A couple of low branches will do, as long as the sun and the air can get to the fibres. A thrashing comb is needed now. A small log will do with a few spikes driven into it as shown. When dried the nettles are now ready for pulling through the comb. They MUST be dry. Even when you have thrashed the nettles into the fibres, once again, hang them out to dry off. When fully dry the fibres are ready to spin.

LOG CONTAINER

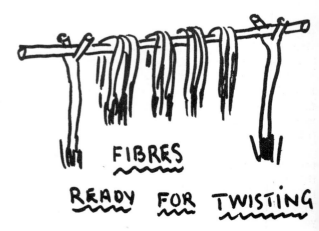

FIBRES READY FOR TWISTING

RUB DOCK LEAFS ON STING FOR RELIEF.

## The Common Dock (Obtusifolis)

**Description.** This herb regularly grows up to three feet or more tall. The leaves are large and crinkly with a millet-type flower. There are a number of species of the Dock family but all look very similar and require very little recognition practice. All may be cooked and eaten in the same manner. The Dock Leaf, of course, is best known for its relief giving when rubbed on the skin after being stung by the nettle. In this, it gives almost instant relief.

**Location.** All parts of Asia, Europe and parts of America.

**Food value.** Very high and sustaining.

**Collection time.** June to Late September for the fresh young leaves and shoots, though if one looks hard enough during the winter months one can still find the odd one pushing its way through.

**Preparation.** The young leaves and shoots tend to be a little bitter after one boiling so I recommend at least three boilings; certainly with the roots. With these I found the best method was to scrape them, wash and chop them up before putting them into the water.

A word of caution here. If you are not used to tasting wild fresh herbs in any quantity, then with this one beware, for if taken in large quantities, then this herb has a very strong purgative effect. The millet-like flower may be used for thickening your soups so do not throw away.

## Great Burdock (Arctium Lappa)

**Description.** A stout bushy plant standing around two to three feet high. Large heart-shaped leaves, drooping and flopping to the ground. The flower heads looking not unlike a thistle, showing a purple coloured flower for a while. One common recognition mark with this plant is the ever-popular Sticky Buds. This is the flower head with the many little hooks. Children delight in throwing them at your sweaters to see them stick and cling.

**Location.** Widespread in Europe and parts of America. A very similar species to this plant can also be found in some parts of Africa.

**Collecting time.** Between late June and early August is the best time for collection. The young leaves, stems and roots can all be cooked in the same manner, though I strongly suggest at least three changes of boiling before attempting to eat otherwise you will find the plant a little on the bitter side.

Later than this they become extremely tough.

**Preparation.** As I have already said the leaves are a little on the bitter side when eaten fresh so first try them cooked. With the roots I found the best method was to chop them up and boil them for a while, and let them stew in their third boiling.

## Marsh Thistle (Salsola Pestifera)

**Description.** There are many species of this herb. Some as tall as four feet high while some species are only as small as one or two inches high. All thistles are edible.

**Location.** Found all over Europe, parts of America and in North and West Africa.

**Food value.** Very high and very nutritious.

**Collection time.** All species from the end of May beginning of June right the way through to late September.

**Preparation.** The fresh young shoots and leaves can be collected any time, but the flower heads need to be collected as soon as they are in full bloom. The flower heads are edible and if one works away at them inside one will find a small but very nutritious white milky nut which can either be eaten raw, or crushed and made into a cake when mixed with other herbs. Warning: When eating the flower heads do look out for small insects that always seem to be inside.

The roots when eaten raw are a little on the earthy side and when cooked lose this and become very palatable indeed.

As with the nettle the stems can be turned into a form of strong fresh twine.

## Greater Plantain (Plantago Major)

**Description.** Ribbed, oval, dark green leaves. Smooth with a slight trace of hairs both above and below. Grows about eighteen inches high. For simple recognition skills learn the narrow leaved version first, then the others will quickly follow, for there are other species of plantain which may confuse you a little if you attempt to learn too much too soon.

A common name for plantain is Rats Tail or Indian Foot.

**Location.** Found all over Europe and America, and in many parts of Canada. A similar species can also be found in part of the Far East in particular Malaya and Borneo.

**Food value.** Sustaining with a strong taste of Spinach.

**Collection.** Grows all the year, but is more prolific from May to late September.

**Preparation.** The Young leaves may be eaten raw or cooked and they do need well cooking before eating.

Not only the leaves are edible but also the fresh young shoots and stalks, the top of the stalk which gives its name of Rats Tail is also edible. This is a

kind of millet and is used for making soup.

The roots are edible but need lots of boiling to remove the bitter taste and the amount of root that one gets from a single plant is not worth the effort, for they are very short and wispy.

## The Nettle (Urtica Dioica)

**Description.** Because the nettle is covered fully in this book as to its merits to the survivor I shall briefly give you another description of it.

There are about two dozen species of the nettle family, all looking very similar in shape and colour but not all possessing the common sting that one always associates with the nettle. For instance the common Marjoram is often confused with the nettle, and I have actually been out with people who thought that the every popular French Willow weed was in fact a nettle. In the early growing stages I can see how this is done but once the plants have grown to full height then there should be no confusion at all.

The nettle leaves are deep green, growing from a single stem which when fully grown often reaches a height of thirty to forty inches.

The common stinging nettle is easily recognised by the novice once he or she has touched it and has been stung by it. This sting is a mild citric acid which as soon as the plant is placed into water will disappear, but I must admit it gives a rather bitter taste to the water.

**Food value.** A very nutritious herb, well worth the effort of collecting and preparing.

**Location.** Found all over Europe, America, Canada, parts of Africa and even parts of the Middle East. I have actually found nettles in parts of the Persian Gulf.

**Collection time.** All the year round but the young fresh leaves are best plucked for boiling between May and August. As the fresh young leaves are edible so are the fresh shoots. The roots are also edible but as with all parts of the herb, to remove the bitter taste I strongly recommend at least three changes of water. Not only does this dilute the acid taste it also removes the earthy taste that one will get especially when cooking the roots. Contrary to popular belief, when a tea is made from the infusion though bitter at first one soon acquires a taste for it.

**Preparation.** Tear off the young leaves and chop them up into small pieces and boil. The same with the shoots and roots.

# The Dandelion (Taraxcum Officinale)

**Description.** When in full bloom, a very strong herb with rich green leaves and a brilliant yellow flower. Generally grown about twelve inches high, though I have some growing in my garden much bigger than this.

All parts of the herb are edible from the flower right down to the roots, which is one of the exceptions to the rule, milky soppy roots that one can eat.

**Location.** Common throughout the world. I have actually come across this herb in the depths of Africa and in the desert of the Middle East. In one particular 'Garden of Eden' in the Middle East I came across a great assortment of common herbs found here in the U.K. It appears that this particular garden belonged to an old retired English officer who spent his last few days in this part of the world and wanted something to remind him of the old country so he took along and cultivated an assortment of herbs. In his garden I found Dandelion, Hawthorn, Cow Parsley, the common Dock, Nettle and the Thistle and many others.

**Food value.** Extremely high and very rich in calories and minerals.

**Collection times.** For the fresh young leaves from early May until late August but it is possible to find the odd leaf or two way into the month of October. The roots, of course, can be had all the year round providing you can spot them.

The young leaves may be eaten raw or cooked. I found that they taste the best when eaten raw. The lower stalks as well as the flower heads may also be eaten raw, or eaten as string shoots as in string beans.

The roots, of course, need little explanation for I think that every schoolboy knows that they make coffee from the dried root. Remember that the root of the Dandelion, when cooked, loses its milky sappy form and when used in the form of coffee it contains no caffeine as does the cultivated version.

# Cow Parsley (Antrhiscus Sylvestris)

**Description.** Cow Parsley and Chervil are often confused by the amateur herbalist and indeed rightly so for of the cow parsley family there are many species that help in the confusion and one species which is at the far end of the line is, of course, the deadly Hemlock.

Cow Parsley grows in profusion at the edge of most of the main country roads in and around Britain though it grows just as profusely in most parts of Europe and America. Generally it grows to about four feet six inches high. It has a sweet simple smell to it, unlike its cousin Chervil which has, to me anyway, a beautiful herbal smell, while Hemlock has an awful offensive smell, of what I can only describe as mouse urine.

**Location.** All over U.K., Europe, America and parts of Canada. Just recently it has been introduced into Saudi Arabia as a potential food source for animal fodder.

**Food value.** Good, though this herb is used more for actually giving taste to other foods than for actual food.

**Time of Collection.** The young shoots and leaves appear from early April right the way through to the beginning of July. The roots, of course, can be had right through the year but remember this particular species of herb can be very confusing to the beginner especially when in its early growing stage. In particular when the leaves have died down. The ever popular Fools Parsley and often Hemlock are taken by mistake.

There is no substitute for experience so this is one plant that I strongly recommend that you learn to recognise and indeed taste before venturing off. For safety's sake, I strongly recommend that you follow the rule of three times boiling until you have gained confidence in first time recognition.

REMEMBER

ONLY EAT WHAT YOU KNOW FOR SURE IS EDIBLE

LEARN TO RECOGNISE BY

SIGHT ··· SMELL ··· TASTE ··· TOUCH

## Wild Thyme (Thymus Drucei)

**Description.** A sweet smelling perennial. A creeping plant with very beautiful pink flowers, and on close inspection one can actually see fine dense hairs on the stem of the plant, also along the edge of the leaves.

This herb grows very close to the ground and may require some finding amongst the grass and other wild flowers. It thrives on chalky ground and can also be found in limestone and sandy regions.

**Location.** Widespread in Europe and parts of America.

**Food value.** Very high, though this herb is used once again to add taste to other foods rather than as a food on its own. Unlike the cultivated version of thyme, the strong pungent thymol oil is much milder, so a great deal more is required to flavour one's meal.

Thyme can be used in soups, salads and with most fish dishes.

**Collection.** Early June, July. The young leaves should be collected for the salads around September as the leaves tend to die quickly in mid-October. This is the time for collection and actual storage though they can, if you need to collect them earlier, be gathered in July.

Thyme as well as a food, also has very good medicinal properties. Today it is still used as a throat gargle by many north country folk. It is not too potent and has in fact a very soothing effect and is a mild antiseptic.

**Preparation.** Boil the leaves or stew with your meat dish. Dry the leaves and use as a tea. From this you will find an excellent soothing and pleasant brew.

## Marjoram (Originum Vulgare)

**Description.** A herb not unlike the nettle to look at at first glance, often confused with wild mint.

A tall slender plant about three feet high with a pale pinkish flower at the top. Marjoram grows best in chalky or limestone regions.

**Location.** Widespread in Europe and parts of America and some regions of the Mediterranean.

**Food value.** Very good, used for appetising the meal rather than as a meal on its own.

**Collecting time.** July to October, the young leaves when fresh should be taken in October, but if they are required for storage, then they should be taken in November and from there onwards, for the leaves start to die off at this stage. Once collected they can be stored and dried off. They make an excellent tea and as the Thyme make a very good soothing throat gargle.

**Preparation.** The young leaves when first picked are very bitter and from my own experience I found that they were much tastier after boiling, and with at least one change of water.

The flower may be eaten either raw or cooked. Used in salads they present a very tasty appetiser. The roots of this herb are also edible but I must warn you they require at least two to three changes of water to remove the earthy taste.

It is not unusual for the stems of this herb to be used in the making of fine fibres as the nettle.

132

# 5  First Aid and Medical

MOUTH TO MOUTH

Tilt the head back and lift up the neck.

Once this has been done open the mouth.

Pinch the nostrils and blow into open mouth.

## Artificial Respiration

Once, on one of my survival courses, I did a spot check on just how many of my pupils had had any practical experience of artificial respiration. It certainly shocked me to find that nearly all of them, twenty, had none. They had heard of it and some had seen a demonstration of it, but for the most part they hadn't a clue how to set about any of the methods used today. From then on I set about including several methods of artificial respiration in my courses.

**MOUTH TO MOUTH**
The beauty of this method is that it can be done in any situation, on the spot. The technique is very simple and not unlike blowing up a balloon. The Royal Life Saving Society produce some excellent literature on this system of rescue and recovery.

**HOLGER NEILSON METHOD**
A little more difficult than the above but effective nevertheless.
This requires setting the victim up in a particular way before beginning to revive him.

**SILVESTER METHOD**
Setting up of the victim needed, once more, with the feet higher than the head.

**SCHAEFFER METHOD**
Once again this method requires the victim to be in a certain position. It is quite obvious that you may not be in circumstances which permit you to place a victim in a particular position so a knowledge of different methods is plainly advisable.

Continue as in Fig 3. until the patient begins to breathe again.

Once the patient does begin to breathe again, stay with him until full recovery, if no qualified medic available to take over from you.

1, CLEAR THE MOUTH AND THROAT

2, FEET SLIGHTLY HIGHER THAN HEAD

3,

HANDS LIFTED FORWARD AND PLACED IN THE PATIENTS TUMMY AND GENTLY BUT FIRMLY PRESSED DOWN TO THE COUNT OF FIVE

## Artificial Respiration
## Silvester Broch Method

1.    Clear the victim's throat first, check the tongue is not blocking the passage of air and that foreign bodies are removed.

2.    Place the victim in the position shown. Ensure the face is turned upwards but slightly to the side. Place something under the neck to ensure a smoother flow of air.

3.    Kneel at the victim's head and lean forwards. Take hold of his wrists as shown. Raise the wrists and place them on his abdomen, just below the separation of the ribs, and press down, using a count of five.

4.    Raise the victim's arms up and outwards, continuing to count up to ten so that the whole cycle has taken two counts of five. Keep to the counting and the same rhythm until you either get results or until a doctor arrives.

5.    If you get positive results from the victim then re-check the mouth for vomit, or any other blockages. Of course, keep him warm against shock effects.

4. AS IN FIG TWO

## The Holger Neilson Method

1. Clear the mouth of any foreign bodies that may be obstructing the flow of air to and from the lungs, such as teeth, seaweed or vomit. Once certain that all is clear then place the patient face downwards and place his forehead on to his wrist.

2. Kneel at the head of the patient and place the flat of your hands onto the small of his back as shown.

3. Gently rock yourself forwards applying gentle pressure to the count of five and release to the same count.

4. Return to the upright position, kneeling all the time. At the same pace slide your hands down under the patient's elbow. Continue the counting and lift the elbows high. All this needs to be done to the count of five each time. Still continuing the count and without loosing contact with the patient's body, slide your hands back to the first position on the back, all the time continuing the counting. Keep this rhythm going until help arrives, or the patient shows signs of recovery. As in all cases of resuscitation remain with the patient until you feel he is strong enough to either speak or possibly sit up. Keep him warm and reassure him. Watch for possible signs of relapse. As in all cases, treat for shock.

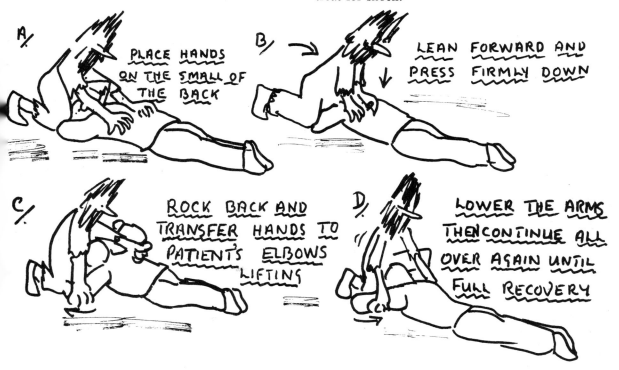

A. PLACE HANDS ON THE SMALL OF THE BACK

B. LEAN FORWARD AND PRESS FIRMLY DOWN

C. ROCK BACK AND TRANSFER HANDS TO PATIENT'S ELBOWS LIFTING

D. LOWER THE ARMS THEN CONTINUE ALL OVER AGAIN UNTIL FULL RECOVERY

## Artificial Respiration — Infants

When practicing mouth to mouth resuscitation then extra care must be taken when blowing into an infant's mouth. This is not to say that you must not blow hard, but remember that his lung expansion is not as great as yours.

There is no doubt that this method is one of the finest ever devised. It is as well to practice a few ways of resuscitation before you set off on any adventure, especially if you are travelling with others.

This is a clear case of a picture worth a thousand words, so study them well. Do remember this though, once you have brought the person around, then that is not the end of it. Shock sets in, so some form of protection must be given: keeping warm, lying in a safe position and, of course, away from any further possible danger.

# Method of lifting an unconscious person from the ground.

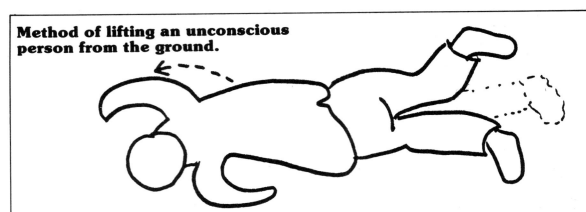

1. Roll him over on to his stomach; place one arm above his head; one by his side; bring both legs together.

2. Kneel at the head of the injured person. Place your hands under his shoulders and walk him backwards onto his knees.

3. Place one hand through the injured person's thighs, holding to the rear of his thighs. Turn your body sideways. Place one of his arms over your shoulder, lift until you are both standing upright. Lower him over your shoulder into the 'Fireman's Lift' position.

**Warning:** This method can only be done if you know for certain that the person you are lifting has not got any broken bones, or any serious body damage.

In any event as soon as you have got your injured person away from the danger area, then as quickly as possible make him comfortable and inform the nearest doctor.

# First Aid Skills

In the event of any injury or possible contact with disease try not to panic, (easy enough I know to say on paper but you must try).

I think the best example I can give you as to why you should not panic is one taught me by a tracker friend of mine who teaches the following rules to his students.

He used to say, "In the first place we are tracking an animal trying to use all our skills and senses, so let's stop here and turn the tables on ourselves, the trackers. We know how the body sweats and also that an accumulation of smells or odours from our personal belongings i.e. shoe polish, hair cream, soaps etc. all help the animal in smelling us out. But what if we had an injured, infected leg? Well, the harder we run the more sweat we produce and the more energy we use, the more tired and slow we become, the more we panic. When we panic we pump the blood faster and sweat more, so it becomes a vicious circle and because of this circle the tracker is helped by our panic. What I am trying to say is, slow down, unless of course you happen to be trapped by a fire, or dangerous river flow, or even at the scene of an avalanche. Slowing down stops you from panicking and probably doing more harm to yourself."

Another first class example is one taught by the R.A.C. or A.A. for immediate action should you be caught in your car sinking either in the sea or a river. Very sensibly they say, don't panic. Close the car windows and doors, but do not lock. Remove your seat belt and let the car interior fill up slowly with water. Place your hand on the handle of the door you intend to leave from or the window you wish to wind down. As the car fills, so the air will move to the top of the vehicle and gradually the pressure of the inside of the vehicle will equal that of the outside water. Once this has been done calmly make your exit, but not before. In other words don't panic! Fear can kill just as well as a missile. Any doctor will tell you this. Overcome your fear and you are half-way there.

This next story I know to be true for I was in the party when it happened. I was in the Middle East. We had been briefed that the nature of the work was such that if we were captured we could expect no mercy and that should any one of us be unlucky enough to be wounded then we would probably have to be left behind, as the patrol must not in any way be slowed down so as to endanger the rest of the men. Well the inevitable happened. We did make a contact and one of the men was wounded quite seriously. On orders we left him, saying if he managed to keep himself alive, when we came back through this way in a couple of days we would take him back with us. He accepted this and set about preparing himself for self-surgery on our departure. We did come back that way in about four days to be exact and found him alive but very poorly. To keep himself alive this is what he had done. Just after we had gone he had passed out for two days, and when he came round, he found that his wound was covered in what he thought were flies but were in fact blue bottles. On brushing these off he found that the pus in the wound had lots of little maggots crawling around, but he remembered what he had been told by the M.O., that maggots on a wound help clean it out and prevent further infection. Though still very sore and weak from loss of blood he managed to boil some of his water and poured this over his wound cleaning off the maggots and pus. Next he burnt one of his field dressings and placed this over the wound, finally wrapping it up in one of his other bandages. The burnt bandage of course was in fact completely sterile and that man's action saved his life. So it just goes to show with a little thought and good survival training you can get yourself out of most situations if you want to.

It will help I think if you learn the Hygiene Cycle. For instance we know the Food-Life Cycle is as follows:

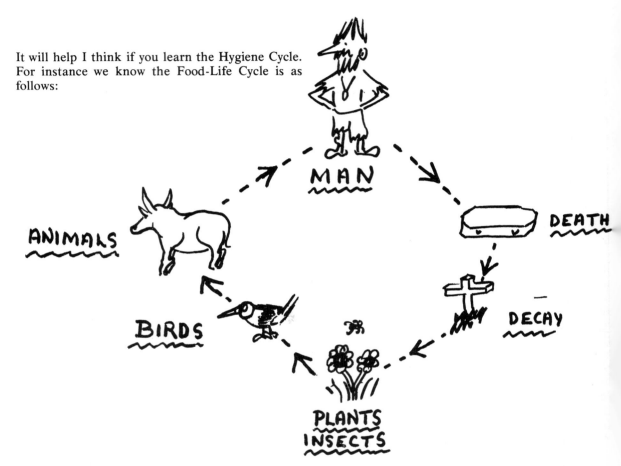

While the Hygiene Cycle is:

| HOW | PLAN | ACTION |
|---|---|---|
| HOSPITALISATION | **INFECTION** | DISEASE/INJURY/MOVE |
| FOOD/CLOTHING/MEDICAL AIDS | **PROTECTION** | DRUGS/STERILISATION/INJECTIO |
| DISCOVERY OF SOURCE & WHERE | **PREVENTION** | SEPARATE/NOTIFY/WARN |
| DESTROY/BURN/CONTAIN | **SOURCE REMOVAL** | DESTROY BREEDING GROUN |

# Simple Field Medicine

## Feathers

Feather

Use as a throat tickler to induce vomiting in cases of poisoning etc.
Use to clean the eyes.
Use to clear blocked throats.
Use to clean out wounds.

## Soap

Animal Fat          Fruit Nuts and Oils.

Melt animal fat down.
Grind the oil from the nuts. Mix in burnt wood, crushed bone and plant roots.
These work as an alkali on the fat making a rough field soap.
Filter through ash/straw.
Collect in container.

## Nut Oils

Coconut

All nut oils can be used as a useful preventative against sunburn and most ground nuts produce oil for cooking/baking.
APPLY IT!     EAT IT!

## Salt Water

Very hot salt water is ideal for bathing the feet and treating soft skin areas.
Salt water is good for treating small cuts and abrasions.

APPLY IT!

Never take large doses of salt to induce vomiting. This is very dangerous to the body system.

## General Hygiene

I cannot stress too strongly how important the practice of proper hygiene is to your camp and if not done correctly will bring you nothing but trouble from the start. For instance, we all know that smells attract flies which carry most diseases; also, other animals that not only prey on decaying flesh and human or animal waste matter but anything else that you may have lying around your camp.

If your camp is unhygienic it can also attract other unwanted visitors and this of course could mean unfriendly man or enemy.

Foul smells are very demoralising to the survivor and should never be. So right from the beginning start clean.

Burn or bury any waste matter you may have as soon as possible. If it is food waste think whether or not it can be used for baiting your traps before you dispose of it and if you do bury it, it must be well down. You will be surprised at just how far down an animal will dig to get to your waste.

In the case of human excrement, then the deeper the better.

It's not too difficult to build a very effective toilet even under survival conditions. This is one of your 'musts' if you are to stay in your camp area for a few days or more.

As well as your latrine, your own personal hygiene is a 'must' and indeed a good wash at the start of the day is itself a terrific morale booster. When serving in the jungle I used to make sure that I did at least three things each day.

1. I washed and shaved.

2. I went, where possible, to the toilet (though I must mention here that because of the situation you are in and the rapid change of diet it is not unusual for a person to go three to five days without moving the bowels).

3. I had some food, no matter how small a portion.

Once these three things were done daily I settled down to a good routine feeling better physically and morally in myself.

## More on Water

Remember, man can go for up to thirty days without food, but four to five days is the maximum any man can go without water, without doing untold damage to himself.

Because the rain forest presents the survivor with vast amounts of water it is more important than ever that proper collection and storage is carried out.

There are lots of improvised methods of purifying water and probably the most common one known is boiling. This is fine as long as one remembers that for boiling to work effectively one must boil it for at least twenty minutes non-stop.

**Warning:** Do not be tempted to drink water immediately you find it unless you know it to be pure. If you have waited so long that you are desperate then you can wait a little longer until you have done some form of purification. As I have already mentioned, once inside the stomach, it is too late for you to do anything about it until it starts to work and remember that no amount of boiling water will take away the brackenish taste that one gets from jungle streams and rivers and by the same token, no amount of boiling will remove the salt from salt water. To do this you must try to set up some form of survival still.

Remember, rain water collected correctly will always be pure.

## Personal Hygiene

No matter which region of the world you may be in it is important that if you intend staying over for more than a couple of days or so, that you make some kind of toilet for the control of hygiene.

I am sure that you realise how important field hygiene is to good survival.

You will need to dig a hole about four feet deep and about two feet square.

Line the bottom with some grass and twigs. This is important, for as the stools build up, then the twigs and grass will help absorb the liquids.

Across the top you will need some sort of support. This is best done in the form of a couple of logs as shown in the diagram. Now surround the toilet with some kind of shield to keep out any unwanted visitors.

When the toilet is not in use it is most important that some form of a cover is placed over it. This is a simple but very effective task, and one that must be done.

Any toilet paper that you may have will obviously want to be dry. So I found the best and most hygienic method was the old army way of sticking the paper on a spike in the ground and covering it with either a plastic bag, or an old tin.

When not using the ash from the fire, a good practice is to throw a handful over the stools each time. This will certainly keep out any ants, wasps and even animals that may attempt to scratch them up at a later date.

Never, never, never just move off and leave the toilet open.

For if you do you are certainly asking for trouble for yourself and possibly others.

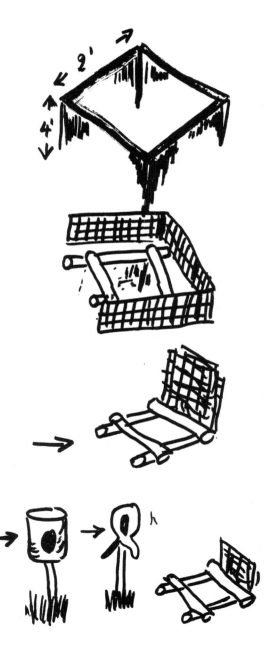

141

## Pine Tree Bark

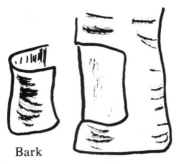

Bark

Tree

Crushed into a soggy pulp it makes an excellent insect repellent.

Excellent foot bath.

Good disinfectant.

Inner bark edible.

Pine nuts edible.

APPLY IT!     EAT IT!

## Elderberry

Elderberry used for making jam.

Crushed with water and heated they make an excellent throat gargle.

Soothing foot bath.

Soothing eye lotion.

GARGLE WITH IT!     APPLY IT!

## Burnt Wood

Charcoal

Charcoal makes an excellent alkali for relieving poisoning and upset tummies. (Mix with a little water).

Wood ash paste will relieve itchy rashes.

TAKE IT!     APPLY IT!

## Sea Weed

Sea Weed

Nearly all seaweed is edible and it all contains natural iodine.

Seaweed wrapped around a wound makes an excellent bandage.

Boil it for a more appetising meal.

APPLY IT!     EAT IT!

## The Feather and its many uses

Once you have selected a good feather, about ten inches long, wash it well and dry it out (under survival conditions it can now be used in your medicine chest). Here I have given a few examples:

A throat tickler. This is an excellent way to help induce vomiting and many is the time abroad I have had to use this method. It's soft, clean and if done correctly will help to clear the throat of any other foreign bodies that may be stuck i.e. bones, hairs, etc.

Of course, there are lots of medical people who will disagree with this emphatically, saying that it is a very unsafe method indeed.

I agree, but it is also unsafe to cross a motorway or make an emergency call in the event of an accident, but if it is going to save someone's life then do it.

The feather can also be used for cleaning out wounds. Once again it's soft, clean and practically painless, but again I must stress that the feather must be **thoroughly** clean.

Once while working in the Oman I had to patch up an arab who had cut himself very badly on a broken bottle. The wound was very heavily infected and full of sand and pus. After washing out the wound I removed all the sand and grit by the use of the feather. Then I had to stitch him up with the cotton from around my trouser seams, after painstakingly picking out each thread. It worked, I helped, the feather came in useful and the arab was ever grateful.

**Warning:** If the foreign bodies cannot be removed by the feather from the eyes or indeed any other wound, then unless there is a doctor on hand extra caution must be used, and if in doubt then do not try to remove.

BOIL AND CLEAN THE FEATHER BEFORE USE

# Fungi Poisoning

World wide though more prolific in European countries.

**Cause.** Fungi produce an alkaloid known as Muscarine Orphallin, which is poisonous if swallowed.

There are somewhere in the region of five to six thousand kinds of known fungi on record in the world. Of these at least two hundred poisonous ones can be found here in the United Kingdom.

Some will cause nothing more than an upset tummy for a while. Others can upset the nervous system, cause dizzy spells and in one or two cases have you running to the toilet.

But, on a more sour note, in this country we have one of the most deadly species on record. This is the Death Cap — Amanita Philloides.

**Symptoms.** In all cases there is a slight tummy upset at first depending on the type eaten, then a slight temperature rise followed by spasmodic body flushes. If the species is the type that attacks the nerves then this will show in the form of mild twitches and convulsions. This generally happens in the first two to twelve hours. Once the fungi has been removed from the system, either by bowel movement or medically, then after a short while the body will re-adjust and recover.

In the case of the more deadly ones then things happen much differently.

With the Death Cap the following has been placed on record. Firstly acute indigestion followed by severe vomiting, headache, stomach cramp, dizzy spells, watering eyes and a general loss of interest. This will include shivering bouts, skin changing colour, reduction of pulse rate to a minimum and a lack of vision and eventually death. This is unlike the poisons from the milder fungi which normally seem to work after a couple of hours of taking.

The Death Cap will not show any signs of actually working until it has been in the body for anything from eight to forty hours. This, of course, can lead to complications in diagnosing the species. For instance, it would be of no value to try to induce vomiting for diagnosis, for after eight hours the fungi will have passed from the stomach into the bowels.

Remember this, the more that mushrooms are boiled the more deadly the poison becomes. Boiling in hot water does not — I repeat does not, destroy the poisons in any way.

**Cure.** For a proper cure one would need full medical attention and certainly in the case of the Death Cap the medical people would need a specimen as soon as possible.

There are one or two things you can try that will help to ease things a little and indeed, in the case of the minor ones, possibly cure.

Firstly, as with any poisons try not to panic, excessive movement only makes the poison pump around the body faster. Keep warm and rest. If available, some salt dissolved in warm water will help, any liquid to the stomach will help to dilute the poison, be it milk, tea, coffee or plain water. Take any of these in small doses at first. Too much too soon will only induce vomiting.

Any charcoal will help to absorb the poison. Burnt potatoes, bread, even wood all help. This is of course depending on how long since you had the fungi and whether it is still in the stomach or not. If you are quick enough with this action it is possible to catch even the Death Cap before it starts to break down in the body system. Don't forget the feather trick, to help induce the vomiting or as many an old soldier will tell you, the finger.

# Malaria

Contacts known all over the world and in most warm climates. More prolific in tropical regions, of course, especially in jungle swamps.

**Cause.** After mating the female mosquito bites man. Once in the blood stream the germs then pass along to the liver where they grow and multiply into millions of malaria germs. All this occurs over a period of five to ten days. Once multiplied the germs are then released into the blood stream where they penetrate the red blood cells. Inside the cells they grow very quickly then burst the contaminated cell. Fresh germs attack new cells. At this stage fever attacks begin to show.

**Symptoms.** Headache coupled with spasmodic fever bouts. Shivering spasms and a rise in temperature.

**Stage 1** Cold, shivering.

**Stage 2** Fever, tossing and turning, delirium.

**Stage 3** Excessive sweating and delirium.

These three stages occur immediately after each other, then may fade away for a short while, thus giving the patient a false sense of recovery, until the next attack which is usually the next day. As the malaria gets a greater hold then the attacks become more frequent, the time between each one becoming less and less.

**Incubation.** After being bitten, normally five to ten days depending on how badly you were infected and, of course, the general state of your health at the time.

**Cure — Preventive.** Move from the source of infection; protect from new infection by covering yourself from fresh mosquito bites. Find a safe rest area and lay up a while. Keep warm and if possible have a good supply of fresh clean drinking water available. Once again without modern drugs available there is very little you can do but improvise. Smoke, for instance, drives away mosquitos.

They do not like areas where there is much wind. In order to survive they must have water. Stagnant water in particular, they cannot stand oils or insecticide of any description. Any of these poured on to breeding areas in the water quickly kill off any new larvae that may be present.

In Africa I watched the Pygmies use resin from a tree and some tree bark to ward off the mosquitoes. In South America the indians use the bark of a tree that contains quinine. Quinine, of course, is well known. The bark is called Jesuits, or Cinchona Bark.

Whatever the cost all efforts must be made to bring down the fever as quickly as possible and get it under control. On no account try to wander off into the wilderness when an attack of fever is on. You will be far too delirious and could do yourself much harm, either by getting lost or causing yourself serious injury. Once the fever abates then, as before, warm soup or milk if available in small doses until positive recovery is shown. Remember you are under survival conditions so it is more than probable that no one is going to be around to help you.

## Amoebic Dysentry

Mostly confined to the sub-tropics and tropical regions. Cases have been known to have started in the deserts and in the Mediterranean.

**Cause.** Contaminated water source, uncooked foods, especially vegetables. Known carrier sources are flies, humans and bad sanitation areas.

The germ attacks the large intestine.

**Symptoms.** As with Bacillory Dysentry, but almost certainly you will loose some weight, become anaemic and show symptoms of dyspepsia (digestive system out of order). Certainly a fever, shivering and a weakness of the limbs as in flu symptoms. There will be a complete lack of motivation and a general listlessness about everything you do. There will be lots of stools in the first day or so and within the stools dark blood spots will show. This is due to the liver having become infected by the germs.

**Incubation period.** Anything from three weeks to a month. Generally shown in a gradual build up process with the number of stools increasing each day and gradually becoming more and more watery. The inevitable fever will, of course, show and possibly spasmodic stomach pains coupled with more stools.

### Cure

**Part one — Preventive.** As with Bacillic, remove all known source of infection and the infected person away from the area. Disposal of all infected food. Protect from flies and other suspect carriers, especially contaminated water.

**Part two — Treatment.** Without proper medical treatment there is very little the survivor can do in the way of drug administering. Complete rest and keeping warm are desirable. As with the Bacilus only warm water that has been thoroughly boiled must be taken in the initial stages. Later as the symptoms start to ease off then mild warm soups can be taken.

One very important thing that I would like to mention here is that if you have had an attack of dysentry of any description then you must report to the nearest medical authorities as soon as possible. This is to see if you have completely recovered and, of course, that you yourself are not a possible carrier.

## Bacillary Dysentry

Can be contacted in nearly every part of the world and in any climate.

**Cause.** Spread by flies, contaminated water, human faeces. The faeces contain the infected bacillus.

Overcrowding, bad sanitation, uncooked foods (especially vegetables) and unclean cooks help to spread the germs, particularly during hot seasons when cooks tend to become lazy and more often than not a little dirty in their hygiene habits. At this stage the bacillus germs multiply very quickly and if not controlled in densely populated regions epidemics soon occur.

**Symptoms.** Mild stomach ache. Varying degrees of diarrhoea. There will be nausea and ache in the limbs as with flu, shivering and a general feeling of listlessness.

The diarrhoea may last for a few days, possibly up to a fortnight in severe cases and heavily contaminated patients may pass anything up to thirty to forty stools per day.

**Incubation period.** Normally one to six days depending on the contact. In the case of the patient being under-nourished and in ill health then anything from twelve to twenty-four hours after contact the first symptoms will start to show generally in the form of mild stomach pains.

### Cure

**Part one — Preventive.** Remove from contaminated source and if possible area. Disposal of all garbage, protection of food and patient from germ carriers i.e. flies, contaminated water. Protect all food from further contamination and all water must be boiled thoroughly for at least five full minutes before use.

**Part two — Treatment.** Complete rest and isolation from all possible contacts. A thorough disposal of all stools by burning.

For the first twenty-four hours or so you will find that you will only be able to take very small quantities of boiled water. However, once able to take the water without vomiting, or passing it almost immediately in your stools, then fresh milk or soups may be taken. But once again, only in small, mild doses until the stomach has re-adjusted.

# Snake Bites

For you to become infected by snake poison you first must be bitten by a poisonous snake and for the poison to take effect in your body then the snake must puncture the skin thus injecting the poison into your blood stream. Not all snakes are poisonous, far from it.

To pierce the skin the snake bites with two horned prongs inside its mouth. Inside the snake's head there is a poison sac. The poison is passed down the hollow prongs and into the blood stream.

**Symptoms.** Rapid swelling and a feeling of burning immediately around the bitten area. The skin around the bite seems to glow for a few seconds. A kind of paralysis begins. Your breathing becomes a little difficult. Palpitations, dizziness, faintness, convulsions and later more sever paralysis. In extreme cases, death. This depends, of course, on the physical health of the person at the time of infection.

**Incubation.** Generally fifteen to twenty minutes after the bite. This, of course, can be speeded up by excessive work causing the poison to move through the blood stream more quickly. Panic is inevitable but where possible try to subdue it.

**Cure.** Where possible apply a tourniquet as near as possible to the bite as you can making sure that the tourniquet is between the wound and the heart. Prompt sucking of the wound to extract the poison will help considerably and should be continued for a good five minutes spitting out the poison.

**Warning:** You must remember to remove the tourniquet after fifteen minutes maximum. If you fail to do this then you could possibly injure the patient and you will end up with a gangrenous infection. Do not tie the tourniquet on so that you have to undo it after use. The correct way is to ensure that as soon as you release the tourniquet it will immediately spring loose for you. This is important in case you should pass out while attempting to remove the poison. Once you have removed most of the poison you will need to arrange some form of dressing, some hot water for cleansing and somewhere for you to lie down for a while. Boiling hot water on the wound is fine but remember scalding water can destroy the cells around the wound as well.

For three or four days you will suffer some discomfort but providing you have carried out your survival skill correctly there is no reason why you should not come out of it O.K., especially if you are in good health.

# Cholera

One of the most dangerous and fatal diseases of the world. World wide, but more prolific in Asia, especially in India and Pakistan.

**Cause.** A germ found in the faeces of man. This in turn is passed into water which is another contact to man and, of course, the omnipresent fly is also a carrier.

**Symptoms.** It shows in three stages. The first stage lasting for twelve hours or so. Diarrhoea, vomiting, excessive stool shows, fever, cramp in the limbs then later in the intestine and abdomen, excessive thirst, bloodshot eyes, sunken and sallow features. A slight lack of vision and extreme weakness all round.

The second stage shows the same symptoms as the first but much more acutely now. The skin becomes textureless and tends to take on a very pale blue colour. At the same time, because of the lack of fluids which have been drained away the skin becomes rough and wrinkled as in old age. The voice will start to break up and eventually, because of the lack of lubrication in the throat region, will take on that of a whisper. At this stage urine is passed as a minimum and deep dehydration has now set in.

The third stage is probably the most critical. Here you can either be cured or die, depending on how the previous treatments have gone.

The fever will seem to intensify, then gradually as the cure begins to work a slow but definite drop of temperature will show, colour comes back gradually to the skin and the patient is able to take small amounts of water to compensate for the dehydration.

**Incubation.** Anything from a couple of hours to a week, depending on the standard of your fitness at the time of contact.

**Cure.** Complete rest and isolation from all known sources of contact and carriers. Burn and destroy all clothing or other materials that may have been contaminated. Boil thoroughly, all water and milk before use. Protect from flies. Keep warm and drink only small quantities of milk, water and as in India, small portions of well watered rice. This must continue until such time as you feel fit and able to take bigger portions, but this will not be for some time.

Without proper medical assistance and indeed aid, there is nothing you can do if you contact cholera under survival conditions. However, if there is any chance at all, then you must take it.

## Yellow Fever

Peculiar to the tropics, mainly found in Africa and South America. It is unknown in the Far East.

**Cause.** Transmitted by mosquito biting man and infecting the blood stream.

**Symptoms.** As with malaria. When severe it comes in three stages. The first symptoms to appear are normally sudden headache, pains in the limbs and chilling, then a rapid rise in temperature. The eyes become bloodshot, vomiting occurs. The inside of the mouth feels swollen and the tongue becomes furred.

At this stage the bowels begin to tighten and the patient becomes constipated. The kidneys become inflamed and tender to touch. When urine is passed it becomes less and less with each passing.

Normally the symptoms last for three to four days. The next stage will occur after the third day when the fever seems to have abated.

The third stage shows about the fourth day. Vomiting is now more frequent and it shows black. The person will now become very weak. Jaundice appears at this stage, hence the name Jaundice Fever or Yellow Fever.

**Incubation.** Usually three to five days but could be eight to ten.

**Cure.** As with malaria complete rest and removal from infection. Removal of infection source and possible carriers. Burn all waste. Keep warm and prepare for a ten day attack. All water must be boiled and available for use. Once the fever has passed then every effort must be made to prevent further attacks and to regain health and strength. Our old friends milk and soup will again aid in rapid recovery and because of the throat infection any ice blocks or cubes available will also help considerably.

## Food Poisoning

This is self explanatory. Lack of proper camp hygiene is more often than not the main cause of infection. Though no amount of personal hygiene will help if the food source is contaminated.

Most germs are killed off when placed into boiling water, but normally when one is under survival conditions one tends to overlook these things. This you must never do. If you have any doubt about the state of the food supply then throw it away. You cannot afford to risk contacting anything that is going to slow you right down or even kill you. A little care and caution will not go amiss.

Prevention is always better than cure.

## Three Day Fever (Sand Fly Fever)

Found mainly in the Mediterranean and sub-tropics.

**Cause.** A small midge fly found in grass lands. Tends to bite you around the ankles, wrists and neck. Once bitten the infection carries into the blood stream. The first signs of the actual bite that you will notice will be when you start itching in the bite area. In return you will start aggravating the itch by scratching more and more. If you are sweating the itching becomes unbearable and in time, through excessive scratching, you will find that you have in fact made the wound bleed and, of course, this in turn only leads to blood poisoning and other infections.

**Symptoms.** Headache, feverish, similar to flu. Bloodshot eyes, flushed face.

**Incubation.** Normally two to six days. As with the title the fever seems to last no more than three days at the most, then it begins to abate.

**Cure.** Lots of rest and complete protection from further infection. Camp well away from grass or scrub land where possible.

A very light diet, with plenty of liquids, especially warm milk or soups.

## Scabies

Found all over the world.

**Cause.** Small insect, itch-mite, burrowing under the skin and laying her eggs.

Scabies is a contact disease and is not confined to any one sex. It can be transferred from one person to another by the simple exchange of clothing.

**Symptoms.** Excessive itching around the groin, wrists and in between the toes and fingers, in fact all parts of the body that are normally warm and protected.

Scabies is usually associated with persons of dirty habits and habitats; people who do not wash or bathe regularly.

If not controlled properly in confined spaces where there are lots of people in close contact, then it can quickly spread and epidemics soon break out. It is rare for scabies to show on the facial regions though there are some cases on medical record.

The little flea that bites needs fresh blood to survive and while the flea is doing this you will feel nothing. It is, in fact, the incubation of the egg that you feel, along with the incubating flea moving around in the tunnels of your skin, that the flea made when it first entered your skin. The male species of the flea only crawl around on the surface of your skin. What with the flea burrowing, the eggs hatching and the one crawling around, they drive you crazy with itching if not controlled, especially if the body is dirty and excessively warm.

**Incubation.** Almost immediately on skin contact. As you rub and scratch so you burst the egg cells and cause further infection.

**Cure.** Plenty of soap and water and the longer you can soak in hot water the better. Pour as many nettles as you can into your bath; this kills off the eggs, as does the bark from any pine tree. It is important that you open the pores of the skin as quickly as possible. Oil, paraffin, even petrol will help under survival conditions, but beware of infection.

The most important part of the cure is, of course, to remove the source of infection. If old clothing is suspected then, if possible, burn it or at least soak it for a few hours, even hanging the clothes in dense smoke for a while will help.

## Field Medicine

Crushed bones of any description make excellent medicines for the slowing down of dysentry. Any type of bone will do, fresh or old. Simply crush down into a fine powder and swallow.

One of the fish experts working with me on an expedition once told me that it was not recommended to try this with shell fish, as certain species were very dangerous. I did not disagree with him though in the back of my mind was a picture of an arab doing just this and, I might add, getting results. I know, for I was one of the people who took some of his medicine and there was no doubt about it; it cured me of 'the runs'.

Coming nearer home, of course, I always tell my students about our own English Oak, the outer bark of which is very rich in the drug tannin, which, as every outdoor man will tell you, is excellent for helping in the cure of dysentry.

The bark must, of course, be well boiled for at least twenty-four hours and with every boiling it is best to let the water drain away each time as with steam. Then keep topping up with fresh water. Once done you will find it has excellent curative powers.

As a substitute, of course, any form of chalk, ground up, will do. Even the good old English cup of strong tea, or coffee and remember this can be made from a various assortment of herbs, one in particular which has a very good slowing down effect on dysentry is the ever popular bracken or dried bramble leaves.

## Prickly Heat

This condition hits nearly everyone who is suddenly transported from a mild climate into a hot one.

**Cause.** The skin's surface becomes sodden with perspiration and more often than not through excessive exercise. This blocks up the sweat glands and does not allow the body's natural cooling system to function correctly. It is further aggravated by the intake of hot drinks. In doing this the body will only sweat more and cause more aggravation, so it becomes a vicious circle.

**Symptoms.** The severe itching and discomfort in extreme conditions can and often does, drive a man crazy, causing much distress, but with treatment and care once the body has started to dry out so to speak, it soon disperses.

**Cure.** Bathing in cold water will ease the itching a little, but only while you are actually in the water. For a full cure you have to dry out the skin's surface and where possible keep in the shade and in a slight breeze.

Try not to wear rough clothing and avoid putting ointments on the body. Best let nature take its course.

It is well to remember that you can get prickly heat in this country just as in any other.

The use of ordinary soaps does not help a great deal. A light dusting with body powder will help a little, though do not over-do it. I have even tried wiping the body with the peel of a lemon or orange. Though the feeling was nice, it did little to help my itching in any way, but I think it would be fair to say that when I tried the melon and sliced cucumber this certainly gave me some relief. Bathing in the sea gives some relief but, as with all water, once in the sun again the itching soon returns.

The Arabs taught me a very simple, but effective, method to get a good night's sleep and rest, and that was to wet a towel with cold water and lay this over your body when you go off to sleep. I found it worked excellently and gave me a good night's sleep. Being raised of the ground so that a cool breeze flowed over the body also worked well.

## Herbal Classification

The following titles may help you when deciding just what herb does what. It is not possible for me to cover in any great depth all the various herbs and their powers in this book, so I will mention only a few on each heading. As I have said before, there are some excellent books on the market which will give you a greater depth than I have here.

**STYPTIC (Astringents)** are medicines which condense and coagulate the tissue and arrest discharge, e.g. tannin, oak bark, black berry root etc.

**CARMINATIVES (Stimulants)** are medicines which allay intestinal pains, stop muscle griping pains and generally soothe the affected area.

**CATHARTICS (Purges)** These medicines affect the bowel functions and increase the movements, in some cases rapidly. Rhubarb is a classic example.

**DIAPHORETICS** Herbs that increase perspiration. The following are well known in this field; Sage, Saffron, May Weed and Catnip.

**DILUENTS** Herbs that help to ease fevers, for instance, the white ashes of Hickory or Maple, dissolved in water make excellent alkaline drinks for the easing of fevers.

**DIURETICS** Herbs that help to increase the flow of urine. Marsh Mallow, Pumpkin seed, Water Melon seed; boil and drink freely.

**EMETICS** Medicines that help to induce vomiting. One in particular is the ever-popular Mustard.

**NERVINES** Medicinal herbs that help to soothe the nervous system. A very common example used by many people today is Willow bark or leaves or Cannabis.

**SEDATIVES** Herbal medicines that control the nervous system along with the circulatory system. American Hellebore and Jasmine, for instance.

**STIMULANTS** Herbal medicines that increase the vital actions of the body.

**TONICS** Herbal medicines that boost the energy functions of all parts of the body. Chamomile, Willow, Dosweed, Golden Thread etc.

## Field Medicine

Should you be lucky enough to be in an area where there are pine trees growing, then here are a few tips that may be of interest to you.

Firstly, the inner bark of the tree is edible when stripped off.

If you peel off the outer bark, then cut a deep notch into the inner tree, you can place some kind of container under the notch to collect the resinous substance that will now seep out. Once this hits the air it starts to harden quite quickly. For medical purposes; for example toothache; remove the soft resin, place it into some cotton wool or soft fibre, place it on the aching tooth and you get almost instant relief. It is not a very pleasant taste but it is very effective and fast. Once the resin has gone hard do not throw it away. Small lumps make excellent firelighter blocks.

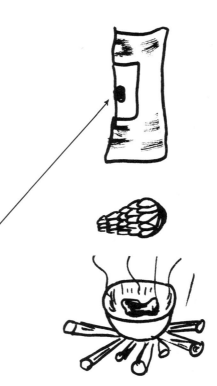

The nut inside a pine cone is also edible and the cone itself makes good burning material. The outer bark of the tree, if boiled for twelve hours with three or four changes of water, can be used for a form of poultice. The water, incidentally, makes an excellent insect repellent. Remember, boiled bark contains tannic acid. This can help cure dysentry.

## Simple First Aid Skills

Anything that you can improvise with, of course, to relieve your suffering is a 'must' for the survivor, even down to improvising with medical aids.

Many years ago when I was studying the martial arts, I often used to finish the day covered in bruises, especially around the ankles. I found that if I immediately placed my foot down a toilet and flushed the cold water over it a couple of times, the pain and the swelling soon went down. Immediately I would strap up my foot with some old car innertube that I had in my bag. This not only gave me some form of strapping support, but it also enabled me to go back on to the mats and continue

to fight, for the innertube also gave me firmness around the injury along with some movement. In other words, flexibility of joint.

Below I show the recognised method of binding up an injured ankle with the aid of a bandage. This, of course, is not the only method I know, but at least it is simple and practical and I found that I could use the same method with the innertube. Take care here, though, for if you tie up the tube too tightly then you can cause further injury. If the bandage is intended to stay on for a long while, you will find that it acts exactly the same as a tourniquet.

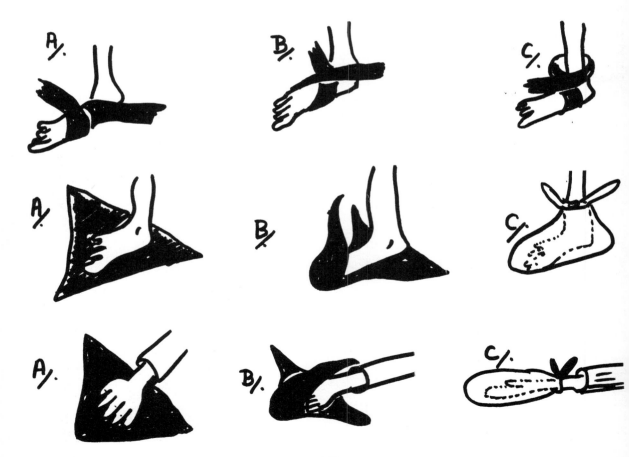

## Simple Survival First Aid Skills

Never attempt to tie a tourniquet to any part of the head and under no circumstances apply the innertube method. If available, use the car or plane seat coverings cut into strips. Most people that I have spoken to who have been in an accident during a survival situation all have had either their heads cut, or legs or arms broken and only one person has had the bad luck to have had his back broken having to lie there until help came. I am not now talking, of course, about the many millions of car or 'bike accidents that happen around the world each year.

A pilot, with whom I spoke about an accident during a real life survival incident, told me that he knew that he was about to crash in the forest of South America and all the time he was flying around trying to find a landing space, he thought of nothing else other than his survival skills and what he would do as soon as he had made a crash landing. When the landing did come he never even noticed that he had actually stopped. His mind was so much alive and thinking that, as soon as he hit the ground he was out and inspecting himself. He was, of course, a very lucky man. Not everyone can get up and just walk away from an aircrash, especially in the dense jungles of South America.

Listed below are a few simple methods of applying first aid to either yourself, or to anyone else who happens to be injured.

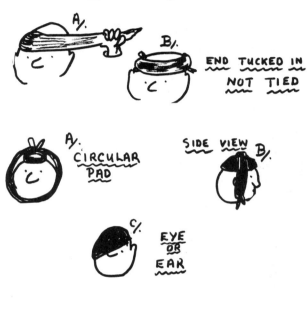

END TUCKED IN NOT TIED

A. CIRCULAR PAD

SIDE VIEW B.

C. EYE OR EAR

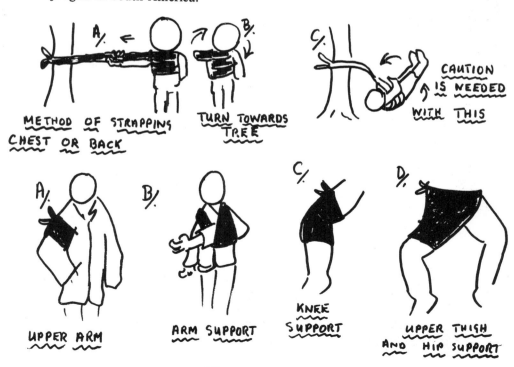

METHOD OF STRAPPING CHEST OR BACK

TURN TOWARDS TREE

CAUTION IS NEEDED WITH THIS

UPPER ARM

ARM SUPPORT

KNEE SUPPORT

UPPER THIGH AND HIP SUPPORT

## The Tourniquet

The principle of the use of the tourniquet is very simple, but I must stress that here in the United Kingdom the medical fraternity frown on its use most strongly; this I can understand, having the utmost confidence in our medical men. In defence of the tourniquet, I can only say that of all the people to whom I have spoken about its use, assured me that it saved their lives. I wholeheartedly agree with them, having used a tourniquet three times on my own body.

In fact, as I sit here typing this chapter, I read, in the local paper, of a young girl who gashed her arm on a window and a lady passer-by who tried to assist the young girl but failed in her efforts to apply a tourniquet. Consequently the young girl died. Not, I might add, due to the efforts of the good lady, but because the lady was not able to apply the tourniquet correctly.

I think the lady should be given a medal for even attempting its use, for I know of trained soldiers who have shunned its use. While serving in the Middle East it was not uncommon to see our Arab medical officer use one when up-country and there is many a thankful Arab walking around today who will bear me out.

Having said all this I must also agree with the medical people, that in inexperienced hands a lot of harm can be done.

When applying the tourniquet one must try to get it as near to the wound as possible, but it must be between the wound and the heart; otherwise it will not serve its purpose.

On no account must a tourniquet be tied and left. The tourniquet must be released slowly, every twelve minutes, to allow the blood to flow freely again. In the tropics it may take at least a couple of times until the blood stops pumping, whilst in the arctic blood tends to coagulate much faster. If you are doubtful about the use of the tourniquet, then perhaps the pressure point system is to your liking, but once again the use of the pad and tourniquet requires some confidence.

Remember, you are trying to stop the blood from flowing from the heart, not towards it.

When the tourniquet is applied and has to be held by the injured person, then it must be applied in such a manner that if, for any reason, he should pass out on you there is no chance of him falling on to it and thus stopping its automatic release. If the patient is sitting up or lying down, then once he removes his hand the tourniquet should automatically begin to release and unwind.

### SEE DIAGRAMS FOR PRESSURE POINTS

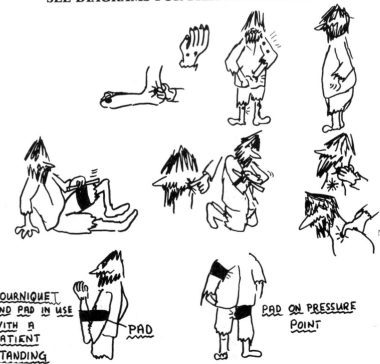

TOURNIQUET AND PAD IN USE WITH A PATIENT STANDING — PAD

PAD ON PRESSURE POINT

154

## Tropical Forests and Jungles

Do not be put off by the word jungle. The dictionary defines the word as; a land mass in the tropic zone covered with a large forest of trees and impenetrable bush, rank vegetation.

I have been lucky, having been fortunate to have actually been into some of these beautiful areas. In some of them I found areas not unlike Hyde Park, open and very spacious, where walking was pleasant and not at all uncomfortable, while in some regions I found places that were impassable unless you had a bulldozer to clear the way; where to walk more than a couple of yards would take you more than half a day or so.

In most parts of the world things are changing very rapidly inside these beautiful forests, especially in the Far Eastern areas. Here man has taken to cutting down large areas of the majestic trees that used to abound in the primary forest. These areas he uses for plantations, new roads, sites for new developments and agricultural areas, but the saddest thing of all is that he only wants the timber and not the land. The cleared area is left and wild, dense brush and weeds take over very quickly, making any movement over the ground impossible without proper transport. Once this happens the forest clearing becomes what is know as secondary jungle or forest.

It takes over one hundred years for some big forest trees to grow to full height, while some of the great pines of North America are over five hundred years old and still growing. Fortunately these magnificent trees are protected by the state and in most cases have been left relatively untouched. Another interesting point here is that, some of these very large pine forests, though not in the tropic zone, are just as impenetrable as parts of the tropical rain forest in Africa.

Earlier in the book I mentioned about the vegetation zone around the world and that it is mainly within these belts that we associate with the jungles we know best. Another peculiarity of the tropic zone is that as soon as you seem to step out of the imaginary line, the forest seems to change very rapidly, especially as one seems to start climbing and it is here on these imaginary boundaries that the word forest comes into its own.

I had the good fortune to be able to live with the pygmies in the tropical rain forest of Zaire when I was on the Zaire Expedition in 1975 and I can tell you from first-hand experience that nowhere have I ever been in any other forest like it. Even in the ones in South America and Borneo I found difficulty in places, but neither of them offered anything as bad as the one in Zaire. The use of any type of transportation was nearly always impossible and by transport I mean the porterage of kit and supplies by animal pack, that is if you were lucky enough to be able to have found some old dis-used animal track, which, incidentally, I found seemed to go anywhere but in the right direction.

At times I found travel almost impossible and at all times it seemed that everyone had forgotten this place, it was always damp, dark and with an overwhelming stench of dead and decaying foliage. Until I actually went out hunting with the pygmies I never saw any sign of wild life, other than a few tropical birds and some ground rats. However, things picked up considerably when I did eventually go out hunting with them. It was the old old story. The game was there, but as I was unfamiliar with the area every move I made seemed to scare the game away. Once I had learned a few simple ways of the forest then the whole area seemed to open up for me.

Do not, however, assume that all the tropics are covered by dense tropical jungle, far from it. In fact, well over half the area is cultivated and cleared. Understanding this will help the survivor immensely. Knowing the location of some of these areas, be they desert, jungle, or just plain savannas, gives the survivor a greater sense of security. With proper training and good planning all of these areas can be surmounted by man. Nothing ventured, nothing gained — that's a good motto from the R.A.F. survival school and one I strongly recommend.

# Jungle Nasties/Crawlies

One of the many things I am often asked about when I go out lecturing on survival is, "How does one cope with the many varied crawlies that one finds in the Jungle?" Well on this subject I can speak with some experience.

Ants, snakes, mosquitoes, wasps, cockroaches and scorpions are the ones that people seem to worry about most.

In all these cases, the ways of dealing with them are very simple, even under survival conditions, when you have no chemical aids to help you.

Most professional jungle workers will tell you that man's biggest enemies in the jungle are, in fact, the mosquitoes and the fleas. The creepy crawlies can be dealt with by either, moving to one side, or moving camp, but the mosquito and the flea will seem to move around with you.

These two in particular tend to bite you and leave their various diseases with you before you know anything about their actual presence.

While the others, mentioned at the beginning of the page, have, in most cases, to be actually disturbed before they do any damage to you at all, if any.

I think, of those mentioned, the one to be most feared is the mosquito. It is common knowledge that this little silent devil (the female in particular) carries the dreaded malaria, so particular attention must be paid to warding off this one at all times.

I think all of us, at one time or another, has been bitten by either a flea or a bug of sorts before we have actually noticed its presence on our body and as we know, this is invariably too late, after the bite, depending on what type of an insect it was as to the outcome or the after-effects.

If I am teaching jungle survival I always like to tell the students, "Look out for the silent ones". Leeches are another crawly that people ask about and, once again, you never seem to notice them until they are actually there on your flesh. But they do little harm to you physically. Women in particular take great offence at the presence of leeches on their bodies.

Leeches thrive on fresh blood, but fortunately, unlike the mosquito, they do not transfer any serious infections to man. These only occur when you panic and try to rip them off, leaving their small sucker section still attached to you and, of course, the next thing that happens is that you start scratching and causing jungle sores.

In the event of you being attacked by a swarm o wasps or hornets, then there are some immediate action drills that you can use that will help you t evade them and possibly save you from death o very long suffering.

As you probably know, they very quickly anger so beware.

One way is to keep very still if they seen disturbed. Easy to say, I know, when a couple o thousand angry hornets/wasps are swarmin around but, in fact, they do tend to attack the firs thing they see moving. If they do make a bee lin for you (to coin a phrase) try once again to dive int some thick foliage. This stops them clustering o your body.

To use water as an escape, jump in and sta under as long as possible, or swim upstream.

Thick smoke will ward them off, but do not han around to keep the smoke going.

If you were unlucky enough to have made you camp alongside a nest, then move, for if you stay i their area, sooner or later, they will swarm and yo may not be ready for them when they do.

A nasty which you seldom hear much about is small flea that bites you on the foot or ankle. It i called a sand flea. This little devil bites you an infects you with an unpleasant disease called San Fly Fever. Its symptoms are not unlike those c malaria, so the same precautions must be taken a with the mosquito.

This little insect lives on the jungle and savann floors and is picked up very easily by man whe walking through contaminated areas. Take fu precautions always. Sand fly fever comes on yo very suddenly indeed.

'Jiggers' is another nasty of the jungle. This is th result of a flea bite around or on the soles of th feet. Once it bites, it deposits a small amount eggs under your skin, using your body as a incubator. They generally take from ten to twelv days to form and fester, but, that ten days can b agonising to the survivor in the form of sever itching. To put it bluntly, they drive you blood mad. After the first ten days you can actually se the maggots moving around under your skin. Don be too disturbed by this. Apart from the continu itching they are doing no harm, unless you bur their egg sac, then of course, things can go wron for you, in the way of blood poisoning. So take car

## Jungle Nasties — Remedies

I have dedicated this page to some of the tried and tested methods of survival cures that one can use if no qualified medic, or first aid is available.

So far we have mentioned, as preventatives, things like smoke, water, swimming, ash from the fire, thick bush and if available insect repellents or creams. Now we come to the part where we have actually been bitten by some of the nasties mentioned. As I have mentioned earlier in this chapter, one of nature's best natural medicines is simply hot water, especially to people of the western world. We have been educated in the use of hot water for our everyday hygiene and we have complete confidence in its use. To us the psychological boost is terrific.

Any form of hot poultice is O.K. to use as long as one remembers that the purpose of the poultice is merely draw and not to cure. However, a hot or cold poultice applied correctly works wonders.

It must be remembered by the survivor that no amount of poultices or hot water applied to the body will give any relief to any blood injections or infections that are already in the body system. The poultice takes the function of drawing the poison out of the system to a given spot, namely where the poultice has been applied. The same applies to the use of hot water.

In the case of malaria or yellow fever, the body temperature soars very quickly, causing excessive shivering and body sweat. So it is important that body temperature is kept as low as possible. This is where the cold poultice comes into its own, whether of cloth or mashed leaves.

Where one has been stung by a hornet, try to take the sting out and apply a hot poultice. This will soon take away the harsh throbbing that one gets from these insects. The same with ants, non-poisonous spiders, mosquitoes and sand flies. Never, never attempt to cut open the wound to suck away the poison. This only tires you out and leads to extra work later on when you have to start covering up the wounds.

Should you find yourself in the unfortunate position of having 'the Jiggers' as mentioned earlier, then there are certain rules that one must follow up if one is to treat them correctly.

We know that the Jigger Flea deposits its eggs under the skin of your foot and it takes ten to twelve days to start developing. As far as is known there is no way of dealing with them other than actually cutting them out with a surgical knife. However, the local population have one or two very effective ways of dealing with them. One is, they are able to remove them safely and quickly using a very sharp, pointed bamboo spike. With this they very gently probe the egg sac, cutting it away from the foot and remove the whole of the sac in one go without bursting it, thus preventing the pus and egg deposits spreading into the blood-stream. This minor operation requires lots of skill, so if you do find that you have some 'Jiggers' to remove try to get some local help.

Another very effective way of dealing with them is to starve them of oxygen. To do this you will either have to submerge your foot in water for about two or three days continuously, or submerge your foot in kerosene. With this method you need a good full day to have any success at all.

Until they start itching, like the mosquito bite, you do not know that you have the jiggers in your foot. However, one way of protecting yourself is to always wear your protective foot-wear and never walk about on the jungle floor barefoot, especially where there is a lot of soft sand, this being mainly on the river banks and native dwellings.

I have had 'Jiggers' and I can tell you from first hand experience that they are not very pleasant. But neither are they something that cannot be overcome by the survivor.

All these nasties are the ones you can see and if you make the effort, avoid. But other nasties that you cannot see, can take hold on the body when it is too late to do anything about it, are the world-wide water-bourne diseases like cholera, dysentry, black water fever and leptospirossis.

## Tropical Forest and Jungle — Travel

One of the main ways of travelling in these densely populated forests is by the rivers and streams. In fact it is safe to say that in most cases it is the only way!

As in all countries around the world, human habitation seems to form up around the banks of all the great rivers and the jungle is no exception. Even the small jungle streams nearly always have some form of habitation on the bank and sometimes even sticking out of the water itself. So for the survivor this is an excellent way of making contact with human beings. Wild life and food source is also more abundant on the water's edge. It is not always possible, I know, to travel down some of the more dangerous rivers but, with a little effort and planning, you can soon overcome these obstacles.

Another important asset to man's survival on the rivers is the mounting of air rescue. It is much easier for a pilot to fly up and down the rivers looking for survivors than to try looking down through the very thick foliage of the jungle below.

The beauty of travelling by river whilst waiting for rescue is that you are not standing still just hoping. Because you are actually on the river, you are actually moving nearer to safety each day. You are also fully occupying your mind and body, which in itself is very important to the will of the survivor once again — nothing ventured, nothing gained!

Remember, all small streams lead eventually to bigger ones and the bigger ones eventually to the main river and, of course, these in turn finally end up at the sea.

## Zones of Vegetation

Understanding how the vegetation zone works is a 'must' for the survivor. Wherever he moves throughout the world the vegetation zones will be there and they do change from country to country, so in order to avoid confusion by trying to explain all the various changes throughout the world I've drawn a sketch of the vegetation zone generally.

Zones of vegetation are belts going around the Earth's surface in which plants of certain types will flourish.

It would be impossible for me to write down all the known species of vegetation at all the belt zones, so the sketch will give you a guide.

The belt zone is not only important to the survivor for his food source, but also for his building material, fuel, navigation aids, personal comforts and indeed his health in general.

Within each zone there are zones of smaller vegetation. By this I mean that most vegetation zones have some plant life that will only grow at the beginning of the zone and not further up. Remember that the vegetation zones throughout the world are all in the region of two thousand feet intervals.

Anything below two thousand feet we class as sea level and this takes us down to the Equator. Just as the zone changes in each country so each mountain range also has its own zones. The vegetation zone of the mountains of Switzerland differ greatly in plant life to the mountains of Labrador, the latter being continually warmed by the warm air from the Gulf Stream.

If the survivor is to move across country for any great distance then it is imperative that he has some basic knowledge of these temperature zones. A good test here is to take out a map of the British Isles, study it and see if you can do a rough sketch of our own temperature zones.

# 6  Survival in the Cold

## Travel in Arctic Conditions

I cannot stress too much, the importance of safety when travelling on arctic waters, whether they are sea, lakes or rivers.

The obvious parts of the body that will come into contact with the water the most are the feet, hands and more often than not, the face. At least once a day one of these areas will come into contact with the wet. Cross rivers only if you have to and use exactly the same techniques as you would in any other part of the world. Always check up and down the river for hazards. Test the depth and move slowly into the water. You need have no fear of any wild animals or dangerous fish snapping off your legs, for if there is one thing to be said for the arctic rivers it is that everything that lives in them are edible and safe to handle. The force of the waters and the intense cold are the dominant factors here. If it is at all possible have the safety stick handy and some form of protection on your feet and when you do cross, immediately replace your footwear and get some heat back into your feet.

A couple of plastic bags tied around the feet and legs with a little water in them before you cross will make your crossing a little warmer because the water inside the bags will warm to your body temperature and ease the stinging cold of the river. The eskimos do this with animal skins tied around.

Without a great deal of patience and a great deal of skill I would not recommend the effort wasted in trying to build a bark canoe. By all means attempt the hollowed-out log, but remember unless you are absolutely sure of yourself then take care when getting off into the water for you will find the log canoe very unstable. By the bank you will feel safe and secure, the water nearest to the bank of most rivers always seems smooth.

Once away from the bank and into the main stream then all your skills will be needed to survive, especially if the canoe is well-laden down and the river is running fast.

People tend to get the wrong impression of the arctic zone. This is mainly due to the many popular documentaries that one can see on our televisions, always depicting violent snow storms and blizzards. Well, of course, these things do exist but there are more sunny days with beautiful sunsets than there are fantastic blizzards. It's the wind that stirs the snow and gives one this false impression.

During the winter months in Alaska, travel is practically nil and only occasionally will you possibly see a sledge or a whaling boat, but during the short summer months all sorts of people can be seen attempting to come to terms with nature. I can remember on one small island that I was on with a few scientists, that on arrival we were the only ones for a couple of weeks, but one day when we crossed around a ridge we found not one, but two other expeditions camped close by. One was a group of Americans and the other from Japan.

By a strange coincidence all were doing the same thing: studying the summer flora and it was not unusual for one to stand on the shore and see fishing boats go by frequently. But don't be deceived by the tranquil picture. Further inland things, even during the summer months, can still be very dangerous. There will still be chasms filled with deep snow and on the higher regions there are still snow cornices and possible avalanche sites. Rivers become swollen and bring down lots of debris. On the mountain side where the snow and ice have melted the top surface very often starts to crumble away and if you are standing on it at the time you may find yourself being carried over the edge or buried under a fall of stone and mud.

Even during the summer months the water will still be icy cold, especially if you camp in the higher regions, so continue to take the same precautions that you would under extreme snow and ice conditions. Obviously your clothing will have thinned out a little by now but even so, do not remain in the cold and wet for too long.

Those of you who have been in the arctic zone will readily know that the winter months seem to come upon you quickly. Certainly not over-night, but within a few weeks. In the Gobi Desert the winds build up almost over-night and the next day bitter cold strikes you. Take note of the animal kingdom, watch for the migratory birds from your area. Notice how certain species of the smaller animals seem to disappear. After all, the environment is their natural habitat and nature has provided them with an inborn sense of survival. An American friend of mine once told me that, as soon as the beaver stopped gnawing trees for his house and food, then that was the time for him to move out, for winter was coming.

Another excellent method of travelling in comfort with an improvised snow shoe is the warm water and grass in a plastic bag method. There are many cynics who I know, on reading this, will claim that this method is 'a load of rubbish!' Well to them I say this; come along and prove to me that it does not work, for I can assure you that it does and works well.

If you are fortunate in having on hand some form of protective covering, a plastic bag or even a simple hold-all, then the next method will work for you. In the case of the plastic bag; get some old cloth and cut it up into small pieces. Place in the bag. Collect some grass or even old tree bark and if possible boil it for a while. Once boiled pour the lot into the bag, then place your foot into it. You must ensure that you have bound your feet first with strips of old clothing before placing them into the bag. Wait a couple of minutes before placing your foot into the bag to allow the boiling water to cool slightly. Once inside tie up the boot as shown. You will find that as long as you keep on walking your feet will stay nice and warm, for heat from your body will be sufficient to maintain a nice comfortable foot warmer. The one disadvantage with this method, of course, is that as soon as you stop walking for any length of time, then the outside air temperature will cool the system down fairly quickly and by the same token if one keeps the bag on for a long period, say two or three days, then of course, the feet will suffer and literally become waterlogged and very soft. After each session with this method you must dry off the feet. Give them chance to air and, of course, with the tie around your foot or leg you must always be on the alert for the stoppage of blood flow. So never, never go to sleep with the boot left on and if there is any fear that you may collapse and go to sleep then think hard before you attempt it.

Exactly the same method may be used on the hands, of course, and this is an excellent method of warming the limbs after one has felt the frost bite. But be well warned, for with frost bite already there one can do much damage to the skin tissues by placing the affected region into too hot a compost

## Snow Shoes

The making of improvised snow shoes is only worth the effort if you intend to go long distances. If the shoes are to be made from saplings, do not make them from dead wood or from too small sticks. Eighteen inches is about the longest you need to be able to move around in comfort.

Simply bend a spring sapling as shown and tie off. Weave a couple of other saplings, but they must be of fresh green wood.

If you have sufficient string or twine available, even animal skin strips, then use these also to help to bind the shoe. The reason why I have stressed the importance of footwear is that this is the one part of the body that is continually in contact with the cold, be it snow, ice or water.

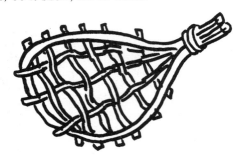

## Traditional Indian Snow Shoes

As I have mentioned earlier, walking on snow in extreme winter conditions can be very difficult, especially when walking in soft, deep snow, when one does not have proper footwear. Improvised snow shoes are a 'must' and, if the materials are around, can be easily made, whether from wood, metal or even old clothing.

Anything that pads out the feet and does not collect the snow — thus defeating the object of movement — will do.

I was once given an excellent demonstration of a simple snow shoe improvisation by some American Indians who, at that time, were serving in the American services over here in England.

One of the soldiers told me that his father was still very much a traditionalist when it came to Indian customs and regularly used this method as a means of protection and travel.

The diagrams show how.

A.  They simply cut off large pieces of bark from the tree. About twelve inches square.

B.  Next they cut up some of the newly caught animal skins, making sure that they left plenty of. animal fat on the inside, for this acts as an insulator. The fur was left on the outside.

C.  Then they tied the bark on to the foot and rubbed the animal fat well into the foot. Next they tied the animal skins onto the foot completely surrounding the foot and the bark shoe, with the fur on the outside, for they knew that snow will not stick to natural fur.

Not only did this method protect their feet from the intense cold when walking, but it also made a very comfortable snow shoe.

Bark platform tied on to foot.

Animal skin ready for tying.

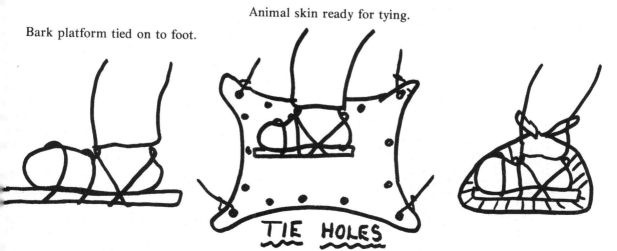

TIE HOLES

161

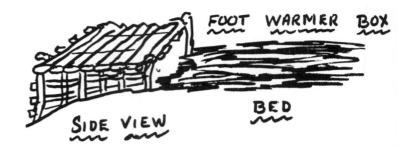

FOOT WARMER BOX

SIDE VIEW

BED

## Drying and Warming the Feet

An excellent method of warming and drying the feet once they have been removed from their wet shoes is to build a foot box. This is a simple task and the effort involved is well worth it, for not only will it keep the feet warm, but it will also act as a boot drier.

For this you will need to dig a hole in your shelter about two feet square. Line it as shown with sticks and straw.

Insulate the box and, if time is available, build a box within a box as shown.

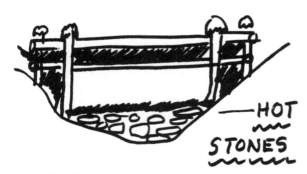

HOT STONES

Place a piece of cloth over the front of the box. Fasten it to the frame and cut two slits in it parallel and one horizontal as shown.

This is important for as you toss and turn, without the slots you will only twist out of the box and lose most of the heat in the first few minutes.

It is also important to ensure that the box is dug with a slight incline for when you do toss around then all the straw and heat will stay at the bottom and settle around the feet. While all this is going on around your feet your shoes or boots can be in the same box, drying out.

Place some of the hot stones into your boots and cover them with the straw. You will find this an excellent method of drying.

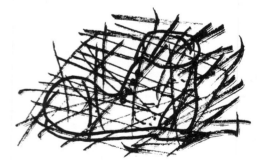

The hay box is also used for keeping your food warm. Get into the habit of warming stones and placing them around your sleeping area. Any food can be uncomfortable. If you are fortunate to have with you your old crashed vehicle or plane, then the problem of insulation is solved, for the seat stuffing, or roof insulation makes an excellent hay box insulator, as do old newspapers. Screw them up and stuff down the sides.

Where possible, when making your sleeping area always try to have at least one side firm, so that the heat bounces back on to your body.

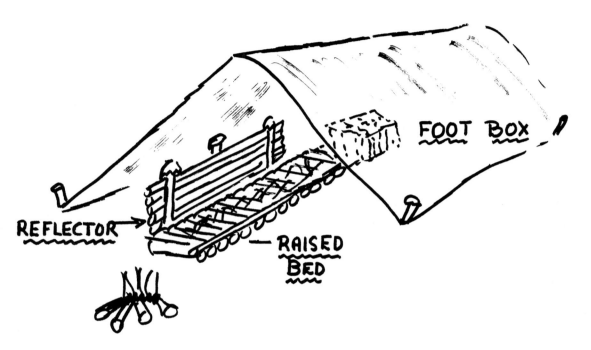

REFLECTOR

RAISED BED

FOOT BOX

You can, of course, use the same system inside your sanger for a sleeping birth. Take care though, certainly use hot stones and insulate, but not hot ashes.

The time and the effort in making one of these comforters is well worth the effort if you intend to stay a while in one area.

It amazes me just how many people annually get caught out though. Just recently I had the good fortune to go along to a well-known public school and give a lecture on survival and afterwards I was astounded to hear of the list of equipment that they were about to take out with them. Not one of the students or teachers had made any arrangements to take along any form of survival equipment at all. The leaders, though experienced walkers here in Europe, thought that the chance of ever using survival kits would never arise. This, of course, made me very sad for on hearing this I immediately lost all respect for the would-be leaders and wasted no time in telling them so. As a result the very next

morning the phone in my office rang and I was pleased to hear the voice of one of the leaders asking if all the expedition could come along to my survival centre and take a few notes. Well they did come and spend the day walking around my static displays. On the return from their expedition they immediately telephoned and explained that not once, not twice, but three times they had had cause to use their survival kits. Not so much as a means of surviving but to replenish their diminishing supplies. Well that is what it is all about. The kit was there for them to use. I have known professional soldiers go out and refuse to touch their survival kits even though they have been on the point of starvation.

You never know when the vehicle or the plane you are travelling in is likely to let you down or crash. Though the main air routes do fly over the arctic regions quite frequently, one must not depend on this for your means of survival. Always, where possible, be prepared for the unexpected.

## Travel — Safety

Parts of the Arctic regions are very rough indeed and for the would-be traveller, going can be very difficult and at times very dangerous. Think hard before you move away from an established base camp. By all means move if you have to, but remember, once you have moved off then it is very unlikely that you will ever return to the same spot.

Movement in the arctic regions can be very difficult indeed, so it is most important that your mode of travel is secure. By this I mean if you intend to use an improvised sledge, for instance, then take care that it is well built and that at any time you can, if you wish, stop it. For once it starts to move down some of the glaciers and gathers some speed then nothing on Earth will stop it, short of it crashing into a crevasse.

Early in 1960 a firm asked me to test a new type of ice axe up in Scotland. I took the ice axe out on to one of the well-known ski slopes there and practiced sliding and digging in. The slope had been well used and though there was a certain amount of snow on the slope most of it was, in fact, ice. Anyway, the first couple of times everything went fine, until very late in the evening when all the skiers had left. Once more I went up and out on to the slope to test and got the shock of my life. For what had taken me the best part of an hour to get up there took me only a few minutes to come sliding down. No way could I get the axe to stick in and bite. I just kept sliding faster and faster, scraping the axe into the ice until I stopped with a bump at the bottom of the slope, which in all must have been well over a thousand yards long.

The thing that took me most by surprise was not so much that the ice axe would not get hold, but the fact that I started to pick up speed at an alarming rate and no way was I able to control it, even though I had the right kind of equipment with me. Now if that had been an improvised sledge of sorts, then I could have quite easily been killed, almost certainly suffered a severe injury.

## Wind Chill

The 'Wind Chill' factor comes very much to the fore during the winter conditions. Ask anyone who has been caught out on the top of a hill in thin clothing just how quickly the body chilled, especially if there was a wind blowing. It happens nearly every year; someone dies because of inadequate protection even during the mild summer months of the European climate.

In the arctic region one has to be especially careful. The slightest effort with excessive clothing will over-heat the body and, if caught out by sudden chilling, can lead to serious complications. So over-protecting can be just as harmful as under protecting. Remember it is far better to wear good sensible under-clothing followed by weather-proof outer protection; and also remember, it is the air trapped between these two layers of clothing that gives you your insulation. Clothing worn to tightly and too heavy will not give adequate protection when needed.

All aspects of insulation and air flow are just as important from the head right down to the feet.

Once you are satisfied that the clothing side is satisfactory, then set about making your living habitat safe and sound and, of course, warm and remember the cold, wet and wind factors. Snow will not always be your enemy. Snow will protect you from other snow, wind and indeed sunlight, but never from severe rain storms. Foliage will give you some excellent cover from most of the elements but remember you must make your cover firm and strong.

One recommended method of getting some extra protection from the intense cold is to try and get down below ground level. This is fine during the summer months in the lower regions of the arctic but no way will you be able to dig to any reasonable depth during the harsh winter months, for most of the year the ground below a couple of feet continually frozen solid and the time and effort can be best spent doing other things. I am now talking of course, of digging into the soil not the snow.

There are many forms of snow houses and snow holes and these can be seen in the diagrams.

If you are lucky enough to be in an area where there is plenty of timber around and other foliage, e.g. bracken, ferns, fallen pine needles, then the following shelters are fairly easy to construct and with a little ingenuity you can build a very comfortable shelter that will stand up to most that the environment can offer. For instance;

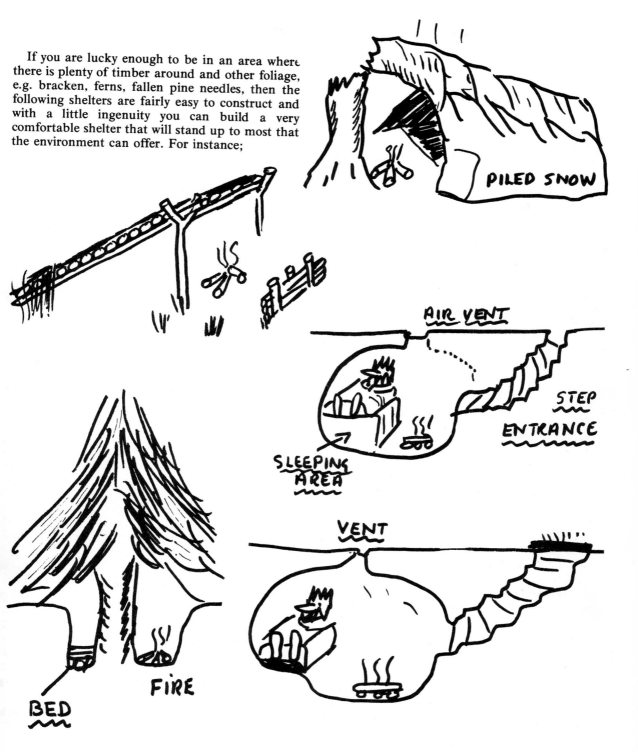

PILED SNOW

AIR VENT

STEP

ENTRANCE

SLEEPING AREA

VENT

BED

FIRE

It is more important than ever, in the colder regions that you are well and truly insulated from the ground, under any protection or covering.

Listed below are tried and tested methods of snow holes that can quite easily be practised in any snow conditions, whether you are in the arctic or right here in the European countries.

THE IGLOO

THE SLAB HOUSE

CIRCULAR SNOW BLOCK

THE POLE TEPEE

LEAN-TO

WALL SANGER

PARA TEPEE

GROUND SHEET

GRASS SOD SANGER

All the above can be made quite simply and fairly quickly if the materials are at hand, but no matter how much you work on these simple ones you have to make much greater efforts to build stronger and more weather-proof protection if you are going to stay in one particular area for more than a couple of days.

An interesting thing about arctic animal life is that at times it almost seems to be tame, for quite often, where man has not been involved in mass killing, the animal life will allow you to wander amongst it quite freely. To the survivor this can seem a little off-putting. Don't think that for one minute you can just go along and pick up game as if it were your own pet dog. What I mean by 'tame' is that some species seem to wait until the very last minute before they either scamper off or just move to one side. The most common example being the popular penguins.

The polar bear, on the other hand, can be very dangerous when approached. Quite often, on returning from a food collecting expedition, I have found them wandering around my camp and I have had to wait until they moved off before returning and assessing the damage, for the 'lovable' polar bear is a nasty piece of work when angered. He will think nothing of pushing right into your camp and tearing it to pieces, just for the hell of it.

All animals, whether from the jungle, desert or even the arctic regions, have a wonderful sense of smell and keen senses of sight and hearing, so tread carefully when approaching them. Just because you are walking on snow, do not for one instant think that they cannot detect you. In the more barren parts of the zone the animals are used to stones and trees falling and the crash of snow falling either into the sea or from an avalanche, but don't let this fool you. They soon know the difference between a casual noise and a regular one.

Remember your survival skills.

Shape, shine, shadow, silhouette, movement, noise and smell.

Where possible always try to observe from a height rather than look up all the time. This gives you an added advantage and as when tracking, try to get the sun behind you, taking care never to make a silhouette if you are on the move.

During the mating season extra caution is needed when approaching animals, especially if they already have some young. If you are unfortunate to be within killing distance of the polar bear, then move away quickly, for as sure as there is a sun above, the bears will eventually find you and catch you out. It is better to be safe than sorry.

## Animal and Plant Life — Food

Setting traps and snares in the cold zones is done just as you would in any other climate and as I have said, during the summer months the amount of wild life for one to trap is quite staggering.

During the long winter months the food source tends to die off leaving you with only the sparse game life left for your survival, so during the short summer months the locals, trappers, North American Indians, Eskimos and so on, trap, cure and store their winter supply of food to get them over the hard months that will follow.

There is a wide variety of animal life, even going right up into the extreme arctic. From the lower plains one can find lots of the small rodents that we encounter in other parts of the globe. For example rats, mice, lemmings, snakes, rabbits, foxes and a terrific variety of bird life. In the larger animal kingdom there is the ever-popular polar bear, moose, deer, wolf, seals, sea serpents, penguins and a very wide assortment of fish life, from the sea trout and indeed river trout, right down to the small shellfish. There is also a very wide selection of fungi to be found in the lower region, including the deadly Death Cap Hemlock. Treat the cold zone plant life with the same respect that you would in the jungle for instance. Though certain plants do give a reasonably high food value, do not depend on them for long for it is protein and fats that you need to get into your system as soon as you can, for storage for the cold damp nights. Concentrate on the plants for fodder, repair work and flavouring of foods rather than as a one only source of food. By all means if it's edible, then eat it.

## Insects

One of the first things that struck me when I went up into the arctic regions with a small expedition was the vast amount of insect life. At times it became almost unbearable for one to move around. I can remember quite plainly seeing millions of flies buzzing around and getting into hair and clothing, no matter how hard we took precautions. Fortunately they only appeared during the warm sunny days and disappeared during the night.

During the extremely cold months there appeared to be very little insect life around, but the summers certainly made up for it, especially during the months from July to September.

Another thing which surprised even some of the scientists that I was looking after were the numerous mosquito swarms. Just before the sun went down, the air buzzed with them and only a fool went about his outside business without proper protection. Though they do not carry the dreaded yellow fever or malaria they certainly bit just as hard and made one itch terribly.

In the lower regions of the cold zones there still can be found the ever-nasty itch-mite or sand fly, and unlike in the jungle or desert, where one can simply remove one's boot and treat, one cannot do this so readily in the colder zone, for obvious reasons. There is also the equivalent of the tetse fly or horse fly as it is commonly known. In the extreme north the Eskimos call it the Moose or Deer fly, while one old trapper I know used to call it the 'Bastard' fly. For every time that he was bitten by it he would jump up and scream out "Bastard". Once again, it does not seem to carry any diseases with it, but it certainly takes its share of blood.

If you are going to wander around during the summer months, then you will certainly need to make some form of face and hand protection in the form of a net or veil. Heavy smoke will drive them away from you for a while, but only when you are actually standing in it. Once away from the smoke they soon return, so improvisation is called for again. As I have said earlier, they may even drive you under cover. Remember what I said about burning pine resin. The thick acid smoke from a good wet pine log seems to work wonders.

## The Will to Survive

In this world if one has not the will to survive, then one certainly will not. If one has the will to survive then one will win through, for there is nowhere on this Earth that man has not, at one time, attempted to explore and push himself to his limits. Not all win through, but certainly some do and when they do they readily pass on information so that others coming on behind have a much better chance of survival.

The world is still full of challenges and as long as man remains on the Earth he will continue to probe. The peculiarity of this world is, that no matter where one is, under survival conditions, nearly all regions offer up the same chances to survive. The climate may be different and possibly the source of food supply, but basically the trapping, cooking and protection are nearly all the same.

Building materials in the desert may be different from the arctic regions and the arctic regions different from the tropics, but no matter where one is water is the same and the methods of getting it are just as varied in the arctic as in the desert.

## Water Production

Snow is plentiful as everyone knows and provides an adequate supply of water, as does ice, though one must choose the right type of ice. Any ice on land can be melted down and used for water, but ice from the sea is a different proposition. Sea ice gives off the best water source. Preferably over a year old. Old ice can be distinguished from fresh salt ice by its bluish colour and smooth rounded edges. Salty sea ice is a strong greyish-milky colour and it is possible to find pools of fresh clear water in small puddles on the surface of larger ice blocks.

People can still suffer with dehydration even though there are plenty of water sources around. The methods of obtaining water are also a 'must' for the survivor to practice. Just recently I spoke to a group of students who had just returned from the Antarctic and I made a point of asking them if they had tried the method of boiling snow for a water supply. To a man they all said yes and in each case they had been astounded at the amount of snow that they had to boil to get one pan of water and even though they had been told about the point of pressing the snow down hard in the pan would only cause the pan bottom to burn, two of them actually went and did it.

The very mention of winter survival offers up to the imagination vicious snow storms and wide open barren ground. It would be unfair of me to say that these do not exist, for they do, but not all the arctic regions are so.

As any old sailor will tell you; slacken off on the sea and the sea will retaliate. In other words, if you do not take full precautions and protect yourself fully, the elements will take over and probably kill you.

Right from the start, of course, the whole emphasis of winter survival lies in the protection of the body from the intense cold, sometimes as low as forty degrees below freezing. It needs little imagination for you to foretell the consequencies you would suffer under these conditions if you were not fully and correctly protected. So proper body protection and insulation is without doubt the most important part of your winter survival. No matter what your habitat or food source, without the ability to move around in comfort, you will not be able to go out and forage for yourself.

It is possible, of course, for the whole of the body to freeze completely, especially when you are caught out without proper protective clothing and right through this chapter I have emphasised the importance of protective clothing and proper shelter. Clothing that has been allowed to get soaked and torn, will help to speed up the freezing of the body. As soon as any of the above occur, then rectify as quickly as possible. This rule is a 'must'.

Treat all injuries as you would in any other part of the world. One good point about the arctic is that the blood soon coagulates. But remember, even with the intense cold one can still get infections.

Because of the rapid coagulation of the blood the use of a torniquet must be treated with respect and the use of snow on a wound works wonders, but not on all wounds. The old wives tale of rubbing snow on frostbite must be avoided at all cost, while rubbing snow or placing ice on a bruise will help relieve the pain. However, if the conditions are of the extreme nature then do neither of the above unless you are well under cover and you have some means of wrapping up and keeping warm afterwards.

## Heat Loss

The exposed parts of the body usually catch the would-be survivor out without him realising it. These parts of the body are the face, hands, neck, feet, ears and more often than not the thighs. See below.

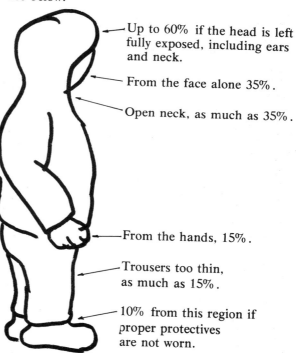

Up to 60% if the head is left fully exposed, including ears and neck.

From the face alone 35%.

Open neck, as much as 35%.

From the hands, 15%.

Trousers too thin, as much as 15%.

10% from this region if proper protectives are not worn.

You can see from the diagram that even if one part of the body is left unprotected against intense cold, just how vital body heat is lost and, of course, if all the areas shown are left to lose body heat at the same time, then it is not difficult to imagine what would happen to you. As I have already mentioned, it is possible for you to over-heat, so a certain amount of heat must be allowed to escape, otherwise you will begin to boil and set up condensation which we now know to be dangerous to the survivor if over-done. Many would-be explorers have found to their horror what happens when they over-heat in extreme cold conditions and they have had to remove clothing which is dampened by excessive perspiration.

## Frostbite and Exposure

In talking to a group of potential outdoor leaders the one thing that stuck in my mind, about our talk, was that at that stage of their training they had not yet sorted out the difference between frostbite and exposure. Some of the party were under the misconception that the only way one could get frostbite was for the part of the body in question to be soaked in water and then exposed to the bitter winds. This of course, is absolute rubbish. Yes, one can get frostbite this way but I can assure you there are other ways as well. Frostbite and exposure are often confused with each other, when in fact they are two completely different conditions. As I have said, there are many forms of exposure and one can be overcome by exposure both in the summer and winter. It can be caused by over-heating or rapid chilling of the body. Frostbite is caused by exposing the naked skin to extreme cold, either before or after it has been into water and it can even penetrate through inadequate protective clothing. It must also be remembered that both can attack the body at the same time, if the conditions are severe.

If you are going into an area of extreme cold, then do read up before you go. The best time for you to study your survival skills is in the comfort of your own home and not on the ground.

There is some excellent literature on the market giving full explanations on exposure and frostbite. The Mountain Leadership Board will be only too pleased to answer any questions on this subject and they offer some very informative advice in pamphlet form.

Another very good way to find out about the correct type of clothing and equipment you may need if you are planning to go out into a cold climate is to enquire at your local outdoor pursuit centre, or camping shop.

Winter survival training is one of the survivor's skills that should not be neglected at any time, it should be practised at every opportunity for right from the start the survivor is at a disadvantage by simply being in extremely cold conditions; wet; bright sunlight; high winds and very severe snow storms. Any traveller will willingly tell you that even in moderate conditions any two of these conditions can kill, if the body is at a low ebb.

Not all arctic regions, of course, are completely hostile. In parts of the Arctic the game source is just as abundant as in the tropics. For example, parts of Northern Canada and Alaska during the summer months, though extremely cold on the high grounds, are beautiful in the valleys with lots of colourful foliage and wild life running around and even in the higher regions during the day it is not uncommon for the travellers to strip off and sunbathe. But beware, for with the reflection of the sun on the snow you will quickly burn. You may not suffer during the day after an intensive sunbathing session, but you can rest assured that you will certainly feel the difference in the night if you do not have the proper protection.

Try not to be caught out. Take full precautions always; remember the golden rule:

**Inspection** (Yourself) and of any survival aids you may have with you.

**Protection** (Somewhere to work from and to live while waiting for rescue.)

**Location** (As quickly as possible find out just where you are, or where you think you should be). Improvise with your home-made compasses and the stars. Knowing where you are is a terrific morale booster and gives you an incentive to work out where you think the search party will come from, or indeed where and how you intend to walk out.

As with all aspects of survival, proper pre-training is a 'must' and on top of the list must be the ability for you to light fires using at least three different methods, not including the use of matches. Without a doubt the ability to light a fire in arctic conditions is a 'must'. Never, never, never consider going out into winter or arctic conditions without some form of fire lighting equipment.

## The Parachute

It goes without saying, of course, that if you are fortunate enough to have a parachute in your aircraft when you crash, or you may have even crashed after parachuting from the aircraft, then you are indeed blessed with a good source of survival equipment. For many is the time when in the 'Airborne' that I have utilised one of my parachutes for comfort while waiting to be lifted out and during an expedition I would never let the parachute I was re-supplied with out of my sight.

As well as the obvious use for cover, it also makes an excellent sleeping bag. I have one now in my rucksack, that I have had for over twenty years and I will never part with it. You can make all kinds of excellent shelters from it. It is an excellent source of bandage. It comes ready-made with a very large amount of desperately needed twine in the form of nylon which the survivor can put to hundreds of uses. It also has, of course, very strong straps attached to it and a certain number of buckles that one can utilise.

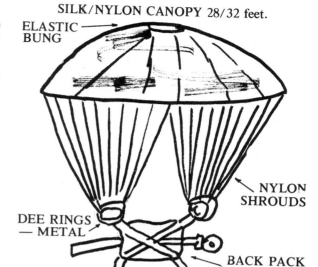

SILK/NYLON CANOPY 28/32 feet.

ELASTIC BUNG

NYLON SHROUDS

DEE RINGS — METAL

BACK PACK CANVAS BAG

LEG AND BODY STRAPS WITH RELEASE BOX

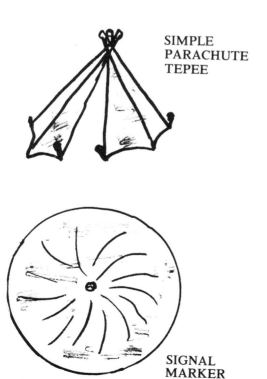

SIMPLE PARACHUTE TEPEE

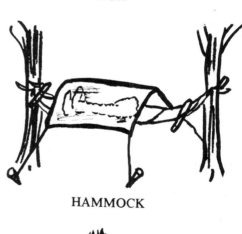

HAMMOCK

SIGNAL MARKER

BANDAGE

**Methods of making a boot/hand wrap from other materials.**

**Warning here:** never, never use metal of any description for making protective coverings if the metal is going to be in direct contact with the skin.

## Survival Aids Improvised from Automobiles/Aircraft etc.

Oil — collect immediately, for cooking and insulating also signalling and starting fires.

Rubber piping from water hose radiator etc. — for burning, storing and making aids.

Electric wire — traps, snares, ties etc.

Battery and bulbs — source of light and means of lighting fires.

Petrol and Diesel — for fires and signalling.

Old tyres — for collector, signalling, shoes.

Old innertubes — traps, tourniquet, signals, bed supports etc.

Lining from car/plane roof — for sleeping on and making foot/hand comforters.

Lining from car/plane seats — for making sleeping bags and body warmers.

Carpeting — ground and sleeping insulation.

Underlay — thermal insulation in snow holes.

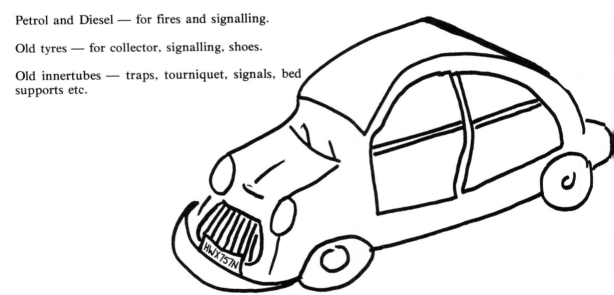

Car seat/plane seat covers — for back packs and other storage containers.

Tools — for making aids, spears etc.

Hub caps, seat belts — water collectors and signalling devices.

Any old paper literature from wreck — for fires and for insulation as well as reading materials.

Mirrors — signalling.

These are but a few of the many items in your mode of transport that you can convert into survival aids until you are either able to move out, or wait for your rescuers. Almost all the parts of the car can be transformed into something that will make your stay a little more pleasant.

# 7 Survival in the Heat

## Desert

It is estimated that there are over fifty large deserts on the Earth.

The largest of these is the Sahara. Other equally large deserts which cover thousands of square miles are: the Gobi, Libyan, Arabian and Kalahari.

Each year the deserts are either growing or shrinking. Deserts 'shrink' because of the take-over by man with his vast need for land for cultivation and habitation. So with the modern use of drainage, water drills, transportation and so on man is now beginning to reclaim some of the land that was, in fact, taken over by the moving desert hundreds of years ago.

But while man is on the move to regain some of the desert for his use, so the desert in its own inevitable way is also doing its share of reclamation. This is done by the erosion of the land used by man in the first place. Having grown, or taken what he needed from the soil man leaves it to the elements to take over again, only this time all the goodness has been extracted from the soil thus allowing it to turn into a dust bowl or dry savanna. Along come the hot tropical winds and the hot summers and before you know it the once beautiful, cultivated land has taken on its first signs of desert.

Some scientists claim that certain parts of the Sahara, for instance, are actually on the move, at about two to three feet per day and for confirmation of this one has only to fly over this desert towards the Congo to realise just how much of the desert is actually on the move.

There are vast areas of jungle, or what was jungle, sticking out of sand dunes and plains. To all purposes it looks just as if someone has come along and emptied thousands of buckets of sand all over the jungle and even more interesting are the river beds where the jungle streams used to flow which are also drying up so that any water that was intended for the jungles below has now stopped.

While some of the vast deserts are covered by soft sand, others, which are just as dangerous to the survivor, are in fact, covered by barren waste lands; miles upon miles of stone and hard rock surfaces. It is in these places that the survivor is more likely to come through safely.

Because of the intense heat that the sun puts upon the desert surface during the day and the rapid drop in temperature at night, (this is because the sky is not covered in cloud), a ground frost occurs causing rapid condensation. This is quickly swallowed up by the dry earth and starts to form in small pools either just under the surface of the desert or, as in some cases, sinks well into the ground. With the coming of the new day the desert takes on its own familiar role. In the first two hours of the day the intense heat builds up again and I have actually seen steam coming from stones around my camp site, caused by the hot sun and many a time I have actually seen a stone move on its own by simply splitting. Those of you who have had anything to do with ice will know exactly what I am getting at. The ice forms inside, the cracks swell and split the rock and ground surfaces.

The more stony the desert, the more water is likely to be around. The survivor must work on the principle that for water to form it must have some sort of a receptacle. On the soft sand it will simply soak away or probably evaporate very quickly. The stony deserts tend to have gullies and dried up waddi beds, these are without doubt the best places to find water and as the diagrams show, some tried and tested areas.

With regard to fires for warmth. It is far better to have three or four small fires to gain maximum heat, so the desert still will work best for you if you could afford to set a couple at a time.

Most deserts get some form of rainfall, no matter how small and every desert has some form of animal life and the presence of animal life alone tells the survivor that some water is around somewhere.

If one is to move around in a desert area and the possibility of getting lost and being put into a survival situation arises, then this is where your survival skills will be tested to the utmost.

As always with man there is an exception. Man has been known to fall thousands of feet from an aircraft without a parachute and survived his fall. By the same token, man has been known to have got lost or separated and come out smiling, but and this is the most important point; those who have survived are very very few and far between, while those who have gone under are far too numerous to mention in this book.

Nearly all the fighting services from all over the world, when working in desert areas, whether in the hot Sahara or the freezing cold Gobi, all give their soldiers intensive training, the British army being one of the greatest forerunners. There must be thousands of Britains alive today who owe their lives to training which they received in the services on the methods of survival, I know I am deeply indebted to them.

All forms of survival training are important, but from my own personal experience I can say without fear of contradiction that the one that tested me most was the ability to move around in the desert with safety and confidence.

The general misconception of the desert is that it is a big open expanse of soft sand with beautiful blue skies, no clouds and oases dotted all over the place. This, of course, is not so — for instance, the strong freezing winds and snow of Mongolia can and do drive men wild by their intense cold continuously driving into the body and sometimes one does not see the sun for weeks on end, while in the hot deserts the wind, equally as strong, can drive a man mad with the intense heat and dust and his inability to find, or even construct some form of shelter. As I have already said, each one has its own peculiarities and must be learned by the survivor, either the hard way or by experience gained in practice and learning the necessary skills of survival.

## Desert Travelling

Not all desert crossings are as dangerous as shown on films. There were times when I was in the desert, when it seemed like Oxford Street in London. I remember on one occasion in the Egyptian desert, I saw no less than twenty-four caravans (camel) in one single day and crossing still further north it was not uncommon to find vehicles of all descriptions passing to and fro across the many desert tracks. At the present moment there are thousands of desert travellers from all over the world: some doing their own small expedition, others travelling through some of the big travelling businesses that seem to be becoming more and more popular.

Of course there are hazards in the desert and all deserts have one thing in common: the scarcity of water. This in itself is the traveller's main problem.

I have come across hardened travellers who claim that a man must try to go as long as possible without water, thus ensuring that should he find himself in trouble then he will at least have some water to survive on. While another famous explorer I know will tell you that you must drink as much water as possible before and during the trip if you want to survive. Who's to say who is right? I know this much, I have tried both ways, many many times and must confess that the latter is by far the safer. That is providing, of course, you have the water and the means to carry it around with you.

There are parts in the desert that are beautiful. Like some settings from a film, while others, as soon as you look at them, give you a shiver down your spine, especially if you know that you might have to cross them.

Remember this: you and only you, can decide whether or not to continue crossing the desert and once you have made your decision, stick to it.

To help you, think about the following things before you move. How far will I be travelling? Do I have the necessary aids to survival? Who else knows that I am travelling? What can I do in the way of rescue and survival?

## Methods of Collecting Water from the Desert

It is not generally known just how much the temperature can change in the desert when the sun sets or rises.

Not all deserts are great expanses of soft white sand dunes, with the occasional tree here and there; far from it. Each desert has its own characteristics, day or night.

I remember while serving in the desert of the Oman and Saudi Arabia. The heat during the day was intense and exceptionally dry, while only a hundred miles away on the island of Bahrein, though the temperature was still very high, the air was in fact very humid and not at all comfortable to work in.

In Ethiopia, down near the Sudan border, daytime temperatures were terrifically hot and it was intensely cold during the night. So cold in fact, that at times, without proper protection or some form of cover, one could freeze to death or as near as damn it.

From my own experience I have found that it is practically impossible to get water from hot dry sand as depicted in some books and even when I have been in an area where water has fallen in the last twenty-four hours I still found that it was very difficult to get sufficient water to survive the day, even by the use of the desert still. Throughout the book I keep referring to the quotation "Nothing Ventured, Nothing Gained", the meaning of which is self-explanatory. But, in the case of the desert still, unless you know how and where to set it and indeed how to set it in motion, then you are only going to find yourself with a lot of unecessary frustrations and time loss through venturing to find water.

There is an old Yorkshire saying, "Tha wain't get water from't stones but tha can have a go if'n it'l make thee happy".

I think at this stage it would not go amiss if I covered the desert still, first giving its good and bad points.

## Collecting Water in the Desert

1.    REQUIREMENTS  Some form of stiff backed cover i.e. canvas, plastic sheeting, old tins or anything that will do the job of collecting and holding water without absorbing it. Warning!! Do not use old leather boots as I have been quoted in one book. Apart from the obvious poison aspect the leather only absorbs the water and it is very difficult to squeeze out.

2.    Some good strong stones with round polished surfaces (not rough sand-stones).

3.    Fire materials — matches, wood, etc., old tyres, in fact anything that will burn and this includes animal dung.

Old tins with a polished surface
Car hub cap flattened out
for condensation.

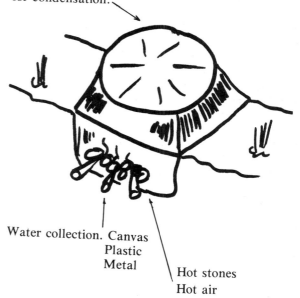

Water collection. Canvas
Plastic
Metal

Hot stones
Hot air

175

## The Desert Survival Still

It is still not quite clear who first thought of the desert still method. For myself I have always been taught that it did in fact come from two young scientists working in America on desert survival work and that it happened purely by chance. Apparently, a plastic cover had been left over some kit during the night and, unknown to the two scientists, condensation formed wetting some of the kit under the cover. As I say, this is what I was told and it seems from there that they worked on the project some more and came up with the brilliant, simple and effective still that they now have. Another story that I have heard is that, during the last war, soldiers serving in Egypt did exactly the same thing, only this time the condensation formed on the underside of their gas capes. This I know is possible, for I have seen this happen. I woke up in the middle of the night to find that I was not only freezing cold but that I was also wet through and the heat from my body had in fact started to work just like the desert still under my cape cover.

However, if the two young American scientists did discover the still then the modern world owes them a great debt, myself included.

The recommended kit needed to operate the still is a small bucket, a length of plastic pipe to suck up the water and a large clear plastic sheet, six feet square.

I can practically hear you all saying, "This is all very fine if you have this equipment but what does one do without it?" Well, there are ways which are best explained by the diagrams.

The setting of the still is like trap setting — very important indeed if you want to gain any success and again the diagrams are best in explaining where and how to set it and where not to.

## How it Works

Once the still has been correctly made then all that remains for you to do is to let nature take its course, i.e. the sun.

For the still to work, it requires the sun to beat down onto it. This causes condensation to build up under the plastic sheeting where, on contact with the under-surface of the sheeting, water globules form.

These in turn trickle down the plastic sheet surface and drop back into the pit. To collect the water, it is important at this stage that you have set the water collection container in the right position, for once the still is working it is not advisable to keep removing the sand seal each time you need a drink. This, of course, is where the rubber plastic tubing comes in handy.

If you do not have the tubing handy do not worry. Allow the still to work for you as long as you can possibly bear it, then remove the water container, take your drink and replace.

All the time the still is working for you, be on the look out for another place to reset yet another one, once this one shows signs of drying up.

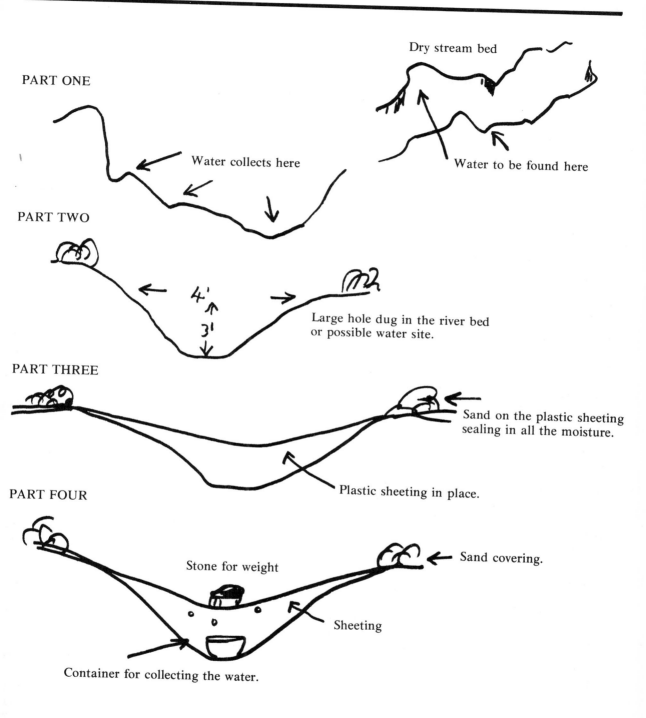

PART ONE

Dry stream bed

Water collects here

Water to be found here

PART TWO

4'

3'

Large hole dug in the river bed or possible water site.

PART THREE

Sand on the plastic sheeting sealing in all the moisture.

Plastic sheeting in place.

PART FOUR

Stone for weight

Sand covering.

Sheeting

Container for collecting the water.

1. If possible line the bottom of the hole with some kind of fresh green foliage. This will help the still to begin the evaporation process more quickly by drawing the moisture out from the plant.

2. As a last resort, you can, if you wish, urinate into the hole or on to some old clothing. Drop this in and this will also help to start the evaporation process.

## Other Methods of Collecting Water

The presence of vegetation does not give the survivor an infallible guide to the best location for finding water. I have been to areas where there was plenty of thick gorse, grass and scrub and I have dug away like mad trying to locate water with no success. However, once I did find a likely spot and set up the still, then a little success was had.

There are certain plants, of course, in the deserts that do hold water, such as cacti (but not all species) and the presence of any palm tree gives a true indication that water is around and should you be lucky enough to find these water supplies then stay around a while and rest and recover. Remember, the desert traveller needs water as much as any wild life that may be around. Look for animal signs also, when looking for water, especially diggings. I have seen large lizards scratching away at the dried river beds and chewing the wet mud and sand to gain water. You can also do this. If you should find yourself that desperate, simply fill either your vest/underpants/handkerchief with the mud and wet sand and squeeze out (Nothing Ventured, Nothing Gained.)

I remember once on a long desert walk in the Oman, while serving with the Sultan's forces, making my way across to a known water well. I knew that the arabs guarded their water hole tenaciously but when I arrived at the well I did not expect to find that each arab, in fact, carried his own water collection skin, so having found the water well and removed the stone covering I was dumbfounded to find the water over twenty feet down and the hole about two feet in diameter. I had no bucket, only my water bottle and no means of lowering it down by rope and it was certainly too dangerous for me to climb down, so I sat a little and thought. I removed my survival bag from my belt, took off my vest, fastened my fishing line to it and lowered this to the water. In a couple of minutes I had not only filled my container, I'd also stepped back and had a good strip wash and removed some of the grime and salt from my body. Later I made a cup of tea, went to sleep, had a good rest and moved off the next morning feeling on top of the world and re-supplied with water.

Once a film unit came out to pay us a visit at one of the camps I was at and they arrived just as I was experimenting with ways of collecting water. I had a good fire going and some large round stones heating up around it. They asked what I was doing and I explained that I was experimenting with two methods of getting water by condensation from heated stones and clothing.

The first one was that I had placed some hot stones into a hole in the ground having firstly lined the hole with my army ground sheet then I filled the hole to the brim with these stones.

The second method utilised four or five old bean tins, beaten out and formed into a square in the sand, shiny side down.

(This experiment works best, by the way, in the cooler seasons of the desert).

Having done this I placed a few of the hot stones under the tins and waited for the cool of the evening and the sun to set, which would be in a few hours.

I left the experiments working during the night and just before first light I inspected them and found to my delight that about half a cupful of water had collected in my gas cape and under the tins, the stones, which had now cooled down, were covered in water droplets and so was the underside of the tins. Both had worked and in each case with a little more thought and planning I reckon from the two I could have got just under a teacup full of water, especially if I had placed something under the tins to collect the water on, i.e. a vest or handkerchief or something of that kind.

## Drinking Water from Urine

I was taught this method by a member of one of the armed forces that I had the good fortune to be working with in the Middle East.

Not only is it possible for you to get some drinking water from your urine, but it is also possible for you to get a good supply from your vehicle radiator, whether or not it is topped up with anti-freeze or any other chemical.

For this method to work you will require a fire, something to catch the water droplets in and a container of sorts to boil the water in.

The beauty of this method is that the still can be made to work at any time of the day or night.

It is not necessary to have the sun to start the evaporation process, though if you do not then you will have to keep your fire going until you have got from the boiling urine the required amount of fresh water.

Basically all it is, is a version of the old fashioned whisky still.

A hole is dug for the fire and another set out as in the normal desert still. The two holes need to be alongside each other but about twelve inches apart. Between the holes you will need some form of a tunnel. I was shown how to use one of the radiator hoses, as in the diagram.

It is important that when you start the boiling process the steam is directed along the hose tunnel and allowed to cross into the basic desert still. Once here the normal action of condensation will occur, only from the boiling urine. You will be surprised just how quickly the water droplets begin to form. I know when I first saw mine working, my morale soon shot sky high.

This is a first class task for you to have a practice on here in the U.K. Whenever possible I let the Boy Scouts and the various schools that I talk to, have a go.

I found that the desert burner worked best for me and I also found that I needed some form of a cover to direct the steam, otherwise it will only rise straight up with the smoke from the fire. This was not so difficult; I simply used some of my silver tin foil that I always carry around with me. But you can soon improvise with something from the vehicle bodywork.

It is not necessary for the hole in which you have the fire to be covered. You will need to let the smoke away anyway.

Remember this: Boiling water will not always completely destroy all the germs in it, so this method is another way of playing safe with your water supply.

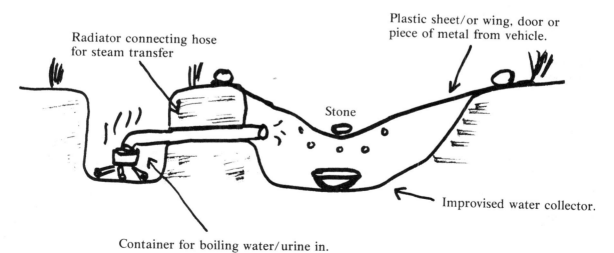

Radiator connecting hose for steam transfer

Plastic sheet/or wing, door or piece of metal from vehicle.

Stone

Improvised water collector.

Container for boiling water/urine in.
Desert burner/oil/petrol/sand.

## Methods of Getting Water from a Mud Pool

CLOTHING

Dig well down into the mud surface until the mud becomes murky.

Using some of your clothing as an absorbent i.e. handkerchief, underpants or vest, place over the murky water surface and soak up the water, ring out gently into either a container or drink immediately.

Another method of drinking water from a mud hole is to dig until the water appears or shows murky. Using some grass as a filter place this on the surface. Improvise some form of tube, place this on the grass, pressing down into the mud, making sure the end is covered. Suck until the murky water comes through. Do not worry about the mud, spit the water into a container and allow to settle. Very soon you will have a reasonably sized drink, once the mud has settled.

If you are very thirsty, take a handful of sand or mud and allow to rest in your mouth.

Once in the Oman a desert traveller told me that this is one arab method of curing the runs.

GRASS

TUBE

CONTAINER FOR COLLECTING WATER AND MUD

## Daily Water Requirements to Maintain Water Balance

| Mean Temp. Degrees Fahrenheit | Pints per 24 hours |
|---|---|
| 95 | 9 |
| 90 | 6½ |
| 85 | 4½ |
| 80 | 2½ |
| 75 | 2 |

The figures shown above are only an approximate guide as listed by the training manual of survival by PAM (Air) 225 this is an excellent book and well worth acquiring if you have the chance. This book, though small, has a wealth of knowledge and excellent up-to-date information that the survivor needs if he is to move around in desert areas.

The amount of water quoted by the experts that can be drawn from a good working desert still is, in the region of about two, to three pints a week. This is, of course, exceptional and requires lots of patience waiting for the water to come. But by moving around in the good location then it is possible.

As the seasons come i.e. the hot season, the humid and the dry, then these figures will fluctuate. So it is as well for the survivor to understand some of the changing weather conditions of the deserts.

## Sand Storms

In the event of you being caught in a sand storm, have no fear. The stories bandied around about people and animals being buried alive are simply not true.

Normally the storms last for a couple of days or so and then quickly die down, so simply take what precautions you can i.e. turn your eyes and face away from the storm and rest. If you have some form of protection cover yourself and sit the storm out. Have no fear, you will not be covered or buried alive. For a sand storm to do just this you would need to be in one spot for a couple of years or so because as the changing winds blow so do the sand formations.

One very important thing though is, no matter how tired you may feel when the storm comes upon you, ensure that you mark the direction of your travel before you lay up. Either with stones, scratches or sticks. Once the storm has passed any trail that you may have been following may have disappeared.

## IMPROVISED DIRECTION MARKERS

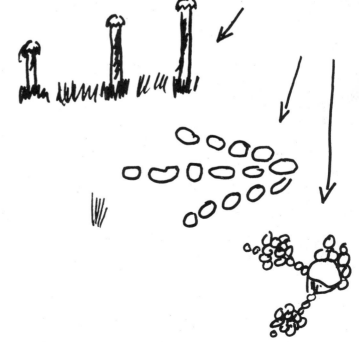

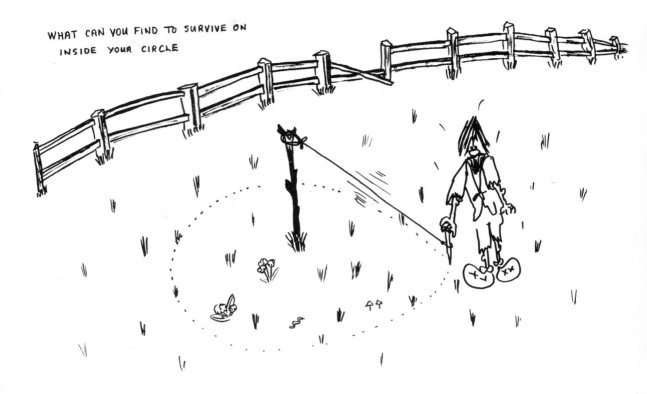

WHAT CAN YOU FIND TO SURVIVE ON INSIDE YOUR CIRCLE

## Final Remarks

I made it a point on my travels to take particular notice of the many varied and different ways of building protective cover from the natural surroundings available. Using an old cliche, A picture is worth a thousand words, I think the diagrams here will help to explain things more simply than any words.

Self protection is the most important part of survival teaching as well as the obvious protection requirements, having somewhere to come back to and to feel safe and protected in is, without doubt, a terrific morale booster. Having a base, of sorts, to work from, build things in and indeed look after, helps the survivor to overcome one of the survivor's worst enemies; boredom. Should you ever be unlucky enough to be in a situation where you need to be rescued you will be surprised just how quickly the first couple of days passes when trying to establish yourself with a home of sorts. Of course the situation you are in depends on the amount of effort you put into it. Finding materials in the jungle is no problem while in the desert things are a little scarcer.

Many people to whom I have spoken say that they know all about building an igloo out of snow but admit that they have never attempted it. I'm not saying for one moment that they would not be able to make an igloo. What I am trying to say is that like so many things about survival training, they have read somewhere about these things but never had the chance to actually practice them. I suspect in lots of cases they just did not have the confidence to try.

Again and again I say, practise when and where you can. Set yourself a little test; for example, pick a nice summer day and see if you can light a fire without the aid of matches by either using the stick rubbing method or the reflector way. Try sitting in the centre of a field, stick a stick in the ground, tie a length of string about twelve feet long to the stick and mark a large circle. From within the circle see how much in the way of survival you can get from it (food, building materials, traps, aids, fuel etc.) This is an excellent way of making yourself aware of what is around you.

# 8 Index

# Bibliography

"**ANIMAL TRAPS AND TRAPPING**" by James A. Bateman B.Sc. M.Biol. A.M.A. published in 1971/73/76 by David & Charles (Pub.) Ltd., Brunei House, Newton Abbot, Devon.

"**SURVIVAL FOR YOUNG PEOPLE**" by Anthony Greenbank, published in 1975 by George G. Harrap & Co. Ltd., 182/184 High Holborn, London.

"**THE ILLUSTRATED HERBAL HANDBOOK**" by Juliette De-Bairacli Levey, published in 1974 by Faber & Faber Ltd., 3 Queen Square, London.

"**FOOD FOR FREE**" by Richard Mabey, published in 1972 by William Collins, Sons Ltd. & Co., London.

"**THE CONCISE BRITISH FLORA IN COLOUR**" by Martin W. Keble, published in 1965 by Michael Joseph.

"**WILD FLOWERS**" by Francesca Greenoak, published in 1977 by McDonald Educational Ltd., London.

"**BE A NATURE DETECTIVE**" by Maxwell Knight, published in 1968 by Frederick Warne & Co. Ltd., London.

"**MUSHROOMS AND OTHER FUNGI**" by Augusto Rinaldi and Vassili Tyndalo, published in 1972 by The Hamlyn Pub. Group Ltd., London.

"**WILD FLOWERS OF BRITAIN AND NORTHERN EUROPE**" by Richard Fitter, Alastair Fitter and Marjorie Blamey, published in 1974 by William Collins, Sons & Co. Ltd., London.

"**CAMPING AND WOODCRAFT**" by Kephart, published in 1921 and 1952 by McMillan Coy, New York.

"**THE SURVIVAL BOOK**" by Paul H. Nesbit, Alonzo W. Pond and William H. Allen, published in 195 by D. Van Nostrand Co. Inc., 358 Kensington High St., London.

"**STAY ALIVE**" by McGee, Lowan, published in 1979 by Corgi Books for Trident Television.